Grade 4

Summer Skills
For the Child Going into Fourth Grade

Written by **Shannon Keeley**

Illustrations by **Clive Scruton**

FlashKids
An imprint of Sterling Children's Books

FLASH KIDS, STERLING, and the distinctive Sterling logo are registered trademarks of Sterling Publishing Co., Inc.

Published by Sterling Publishing Co., Inc.
387 Park Avenue South, New York, NY 10016
Text and illustrations © 2005 by Flash Kids
Distributed in Canada by Sterling Publishing
c/o Canadian Manda Group, 165 Dufferin Street
Toronto, Ontario, Canada M6K 3H6
Distributed in the United Kingdom by GMC Distribution Services
Castle Place, 166 High Street, Lewes, East Sussex, England BN7 1XU
Distributed in Australia by Capricorn Link (Australia) Pty. Ltd.
P.O. Box 704, Windsor, NSW 2756, Australia

Sterling ISBN 978-1-4114-3413-4

Manufactured in Canada

Lot #:
2 4 6 8 10 9 7 5 3 1
03/10

For information about custom editions, special sales, premium and corporate purchases, please contact Sterling Special Sales Department at 800-805-5489 or specialsales@sterlingpublishing.com.

Cover design and production by Mada Design, Inc.

DEAR PARENT,

Your child is out of school for the summer, but this doesn't mean that learning has to stop! In fact, reinforcing academic skills in the summer months will help your child succeed during the next school year. This Summer Skills workbook provides activities to keep your child engaged in all the subject areas—Language Arts, Math, Social Studies, and Science— during the summer months. The activities increase in difficulty as the book progresses by reviewing what your child learned in third grade and then introducing skills for fourth grade. This will help build your child's confidence and help him or her get excited for the new school year!

As you and your child go through the book, look for "Fast Fact" or "On Your Own" features that build upon the theme or activity on each page. At the back of this book you'll find a comprehensive reading list. Keep your child interested in reading by providing some or all of the books on the list for your child to read. You will also find a list of suggested summer projects at the back of this book. These are fun activities for you and your child to complete together. Use all of these special features to continue exploring and learning about different concepts all summer long!

As your child completes the activities in this book, shower him or her with encouragement and praise. You can feel good knowing that you are taking an active and important role in your child's education. Helping your child complete the activities in this book provides him or her with an excellent example—that you value learning, every day! Have a wonderful summer, and most of all, have fun learning together!

TABLE OF CONTENTS

WORD FAMILY TREE

Use the letters and word endings to build each word. The first one is done for you.

		ight	**ace**
1.	l	light	lace
2.	f		
3.	r		
4.	pl		
5.	br		

Look for the letters **ight** and **ace** in the words below.
Circle the letters **ight** and put a square around the letters **ace**.

6. tightrope

7. alright

8. fireplace

9. tonight

10. shoelace

11. graceful

12. frightened

13. placemat

ON YOUR OWN
A family tree is a chart that shows how all the members of your family are related. Write down the names of all the family members you can think of. Then have your parents help you organize the names on a family tree!

BRIGHT IDEAS

Each sentence below matches a picture. Copy each sentence beneath the picture that matches it.

Sunlight can be blocked to create shadows.

Light travels in a straight line.

Light is reflected from mirrors and other surfaces.

Sunlight contains all the colors of the rainbow.

ON YOUR OWN

You can make your own shadows! Cut a piece of cardboard into different shapes. Take the shapes outside and hold them up in the sunlight. Notice the size of each shadow compared to the size of the cardboard.

1.

2.

Light is reflected from
mirrors and other surfaces.

_____

3.

4.

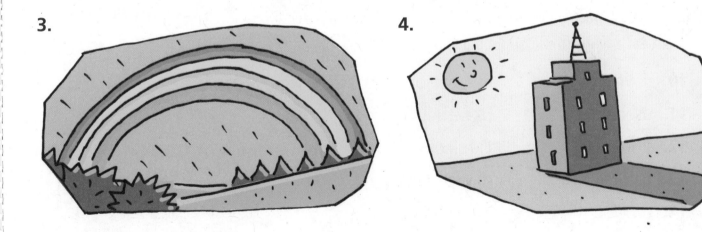

_____

_____

ADDING ON

A **prefix** is a word part added to the beginning of a word. Write the correct prefix to complete each word.

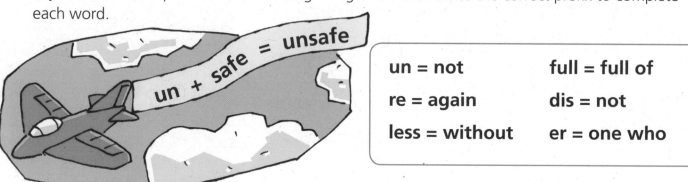

un + safe = unsafe

un = not	full = full of
re = again	dis = not
less = without	er = one who

1. My dinner got cold, so I need to ____re____heat it.

2. When my best friend moved away, I felt _____happy.

3. I need to _____view the book again before the test.

4. I use my key to _____lock the door.

5. I _____like lemons because they are too sour!

6. When I broke my leg, I was _____able to run.

7. I spelled the word wrong, so I had to _____write it.

8. I always argue and _____agree with my sister.

9. The magician made the rabbit _____appear.

A **suffix** is a word part added to the end of a word. Look at each word and its suffix, then match each word to its correct meaning.

10. joyful   a) a person who teaches

11. useless   b) without fear

12. singer   c) full of pain

13. painter   d) without harm

14. painful   e) full of joy

15. harmless   f) without use

16. fearless   g) a person who sings

17. careful   h) full of care

18. teacher   i) a person who paints

ON YOUR OWN
Think of as many words as you can that use prefixes and suffixes. Make a list!

WATCH THE SIGNS!

Complete each equation by writing a **multiplication** or **division** sign on the line.

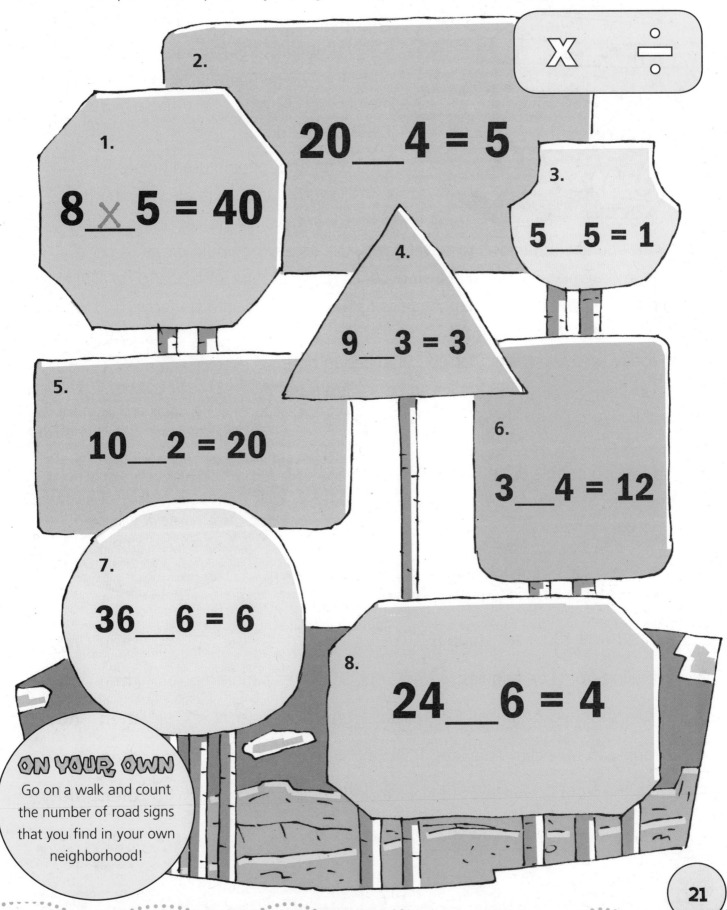

X   ÷

2. $20 \_\_ 4 = 5$

1. $8 \underline{\times} 5 = 40$

3. $5 \_\_ 5 = 1$

4. $9 \_\_ 3 = 3$

5. $10 \_\_ 2 = 20$

6. $3 \_\_ 4 = 12$

7. $36 \_\_ 6 = 6$

8. $24 \_\_ 6 = 4$

ON YOUR OWN
Go on a walk and count the number of road signs that you find in your own neighborhood!

21

TRAVEL TIME

Think about the last time you traveled far from your home. How did you get there? You probably rode in a car, subway, train, or an airplane. Imagine what life was like when people didn't have these modes of transportation.

Long ago, people used horses for traveling long distances. People would ride on a horse's back or have the horses pull a wagon or carriage. If you needed to travel a long distance, you would probably go in a horse-drawn stagecoach. In a stagecoach it would take 24 hours to go 100 miles. If you were traveling from Los Angeles to New York City in a stagecoach, it would take about a month!

Today, we have trains that go 100 miles an hour and airplanes that go 550 miles an hour. Getting from Los Angeles to New York City only takes about six hours. Traveling long distances is easy and fast, so people do it all the time. In fact, Americans take about 2.6 billion long-distance trips every year!

ON YOUR OWN
Think of a special place in the United States that you would like to visit. Use a map to figure out the distance from your home to this special place. Try to figure out how long it would take to get there by stagecoach, train, and airplane!

If the sentence is about transportation in the past, circle **then**.
If it's about transportation today, circle **now**.

1. Trains travel 100 miles an hour.   **then** (**now**)

2. Traveling from Los Angeles to New York City takes a month.   **then** **now**

3. Americans take 2.6 billion long-distance trips every year.   **then** **now**

4. People can take cars, subways, trains, or airplanes.   **then** **now**

5. Traveling from Los Angeles to New York City takes six hours.   **then** **now**

6. People ride in a horse-drawn wagon or carriage.   **then** **now**

CREATURE FEATURES

Each riddle below describes one animal's special features. Solve each riddle and write the name of the animal on the line.

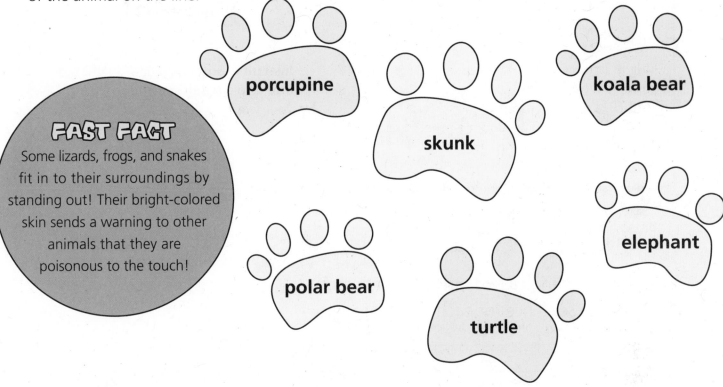

FAST FACT
Some lizards, frogs, and snakes fit in to their surroundings by standing out! Their bright-colored skin sends a warning to other animals that they are poisonous to the touch!

porcupine

skunk

koala bear

elephant

polar bear

turtle

1. I have thick white fur. My fur helps me blend in with the snow and keeps me warm. _____ polar bear _____

2. I have very sharp claws for gripping tree branches. I can climb high up into a tree and escape! _____

3. I have a heavy shell around my body. I can pull my head and limbs inside the shell to hide. _____

4. I have sharp needles called quills on my skin. My quills help protect me from other animals. _____

5. If I lift up my tail, I can give off a stinky odor! This helps keep enemies away.
_____

6. I have a long trunk that looks like a hose. I can use it to drink or to spray water on myself! _____

LOOK IT UP!

Use the dictionary entries below to answer the questions.

bid | blame

big *a.* large, great.
bill [1] *n.* a bird's beak.
bill [2] *n.* a note of charges.
    v. to charge someone for a product or service.
bin *n.* container for storing.

bis-cuit *n.* soft bread or a small cake.
bite *v.* to cut into something with your teeth.
    n. the act of biting; a mouthful.
bit-ter *a.* harsh-tasting, sharp.

1. Which words are adjectives? _____ , _____

2. Which word has two different meanings? _____
   Write a sentence for each word meaning.

   _____

   _____

3. Which two words have both a noun and a verb form? _____ , _____

4. Which words have two syllables? _____ , _____

5. What are the guide words? _____ , _____

6. If you wanted to add the word **bird**, which two words on the page would you
   put it between? _____ and _____

7. Use the word **bite** in two sentences, once as a verb and once as a noun.

   _____

   _____

8. Which of the words below could appear on this dictionary page?
   Circle all the words.

birth	bet	bib	blade
black	blind	bike	blink

ON YOUR OWN
Read a short article in a newspaper or magazine. When you come to a word you don't know, look it up in the dictionary!

24

Read the paragraph. Then answer the questions.

(1) Jellyfish may look graceful as they drift in the ocean, but they can have quite a sting! (2) The sting comes from their long tentacles. (3) The tentacles of a jellyfish carry poison. (4) The smallest jellyfish is about 1 inch long. (5) Jellyfish use their tentacles to capture food. (6) When the tentacles touch another animal, they shoot poison into the victim. (7) Sometimes, jellyfish mistake humans for food and they sting a passing swimmer. (8) Swimming in the ocean is not safe when the water is too rough. (9) Although all jellyfish have tentacles that sting, the sting isn't always harmful to humans. (10) In fact, of the 2,000 species of jellyfish, only 70 have a sting that is harmful to humans. (11) Even if a jellyfish has washed up on the shore, its tentacles can still sting. (12) So you can look at a jellyfish, but don't touch!

1. Which sentence is the topic sentence? #_____

2. What is the topic of the paragraph? _____

3. There are two sentences that don't help support the topic sentence.
Which sentences don't belong in the paragraph? #_____ and #_____

4. Which sentence explains how many species of jellyfish are harmful to humans? #_____

5. If you wanted to add some information to this paragraph,
you could add details about:
    a) which species of jellyfish are in the Atlantic Ocean
    b) the best aquariums where you can see jellyfish
    c) how it feels to be stung by a jellyfish

6. A good title for this paragraph would be:
    a) The Sting of a Jellyfish
    b) The World's Most Deadly Jellyfish
    c) Jellyfish of the Pacific Ocean

FAST FACT
Jellyfish really aren't fish at all! Fish are vertebrates, meaning that they have a backbone. Jellyfish have no backbone, so they're actually invertebrates. Another way that jellyfish are different from fish is that they have no brains.

FROSTY FRACTIONS

Look at the fraction inside each cone. Find the scoop of ice cream with the equivalent fraction and circle it.

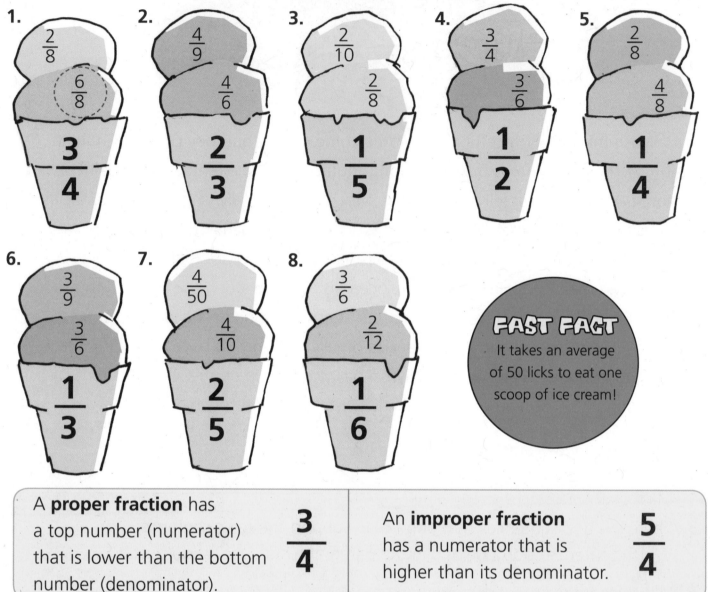

1. $\frac{2}{8}$ $\frac{6}{8}$ $\frac{3}{4}$

2. $\frac{4}{9}$ $\frac{4}{6}$ $\frac{2}{3}$

3. $\frac{2}{10}$ $\frac{2}{8}$ $\frac{1}{5}$

4. $\frac{3}{4}$ $\frac{3}{6}$ $\frac{1}{2}$

5. $\frac{2}{8}$ $\frac{4}{8}$ $\frac{1}{4}$

6. $\frac{3}{9}$ $\frac{3}{6}$ $\frac{1}{3}$

7. $\frac{4}{50}$ $\frac{4}{10}$ $\frac{2}{5}$

8. $\frac{3}{6}$ $\frac{2}{12}$ $\frac{1}{6}$

FAST FACT
It takes an average of 50 licks to eat one scoop of ice cream!

A **proper fraction** has a top number (numerator) that is lower than the bottom number (denominator). $\frac{3}{4}$	An **improper fraction** has a numerator that is higher than its denominator. $\frac{5}{4}$

If the fraction is a proper fraction, write a **P** inside the cone. If the fraction is improper, write an **I**.

9. $\frac{4}{3}$ I

10. $\frac{5}{6}$

11. $\frac{7}{4}$

12. $\frac{7}{8}$

13. $\frac{2}{3}$

Fractions can be written as decimals.

$$\frac{2}{10} = .2$$

ON YOUR OWN
Take a basketball outside and find a hoop or basket. Throw the ball ten times. Count how many times the ball makes it into the basket. Put the number of baskets as the top number of a fraction and ten as the bottom number. Now turn the fraction into a decimal!

Draw a line to match each picture with the equivalent fraction and decimal.

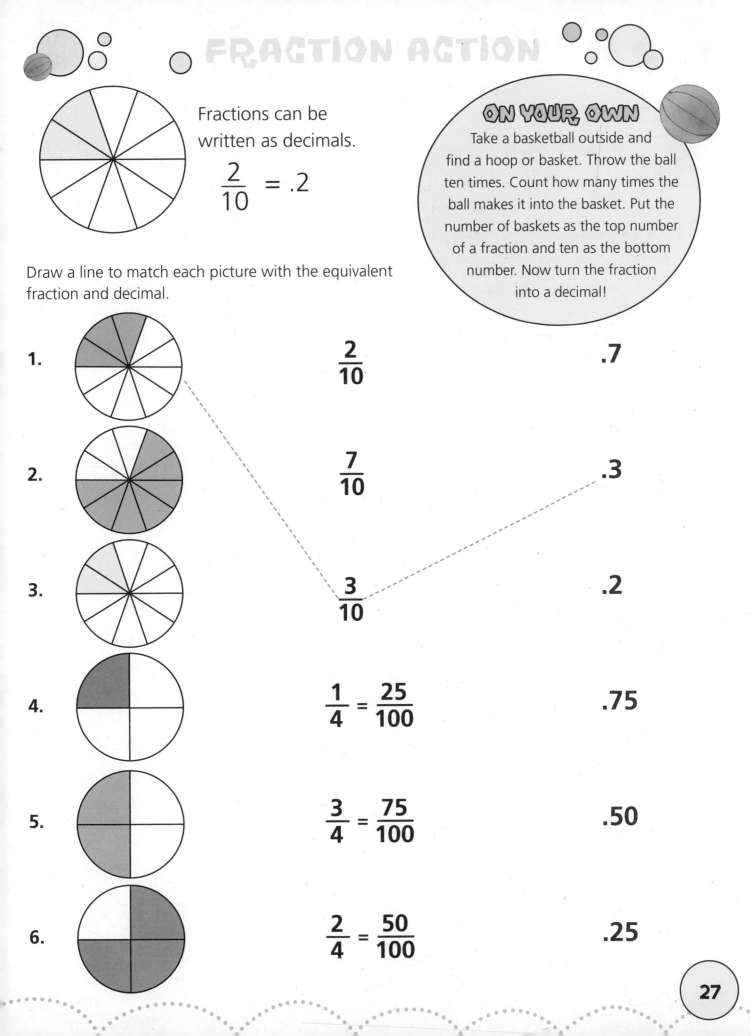

1.

2.

3.

4.

5.

6.

$$\frac{2}{10}$$

$$\frac{7}{10}$$

$$\frac{3}{10}$$

$$\frac{1}{4} = \frac{25}{100}$$

$$\frac{3}{4} = \frac{75}{100}$$

$$\frac{2}{4} = \frac{50}{100}$$

.7

.3

.2

.75

.50

.25

FLAG DAY

The first people to live in America didn't have their own flag. America was ruled by England, so people flew the British flag. George Washington decided that the United States needed its own flag because it was a new country. At this time, there were thirteen different areas, called colonies. So, the flag had thirteen stripes and thirteen stars to represent these colonies. On June 14, 1777, the U.S. Continental Congress declared this design to be the official U.S. flag.

As the United States continued to grow, the look of the flag changed. Each time there was a new state, another star was added to the flag. The most recent star was added in 1959 when Hawaii became a state. The number of stripes has always remained at thirteen, in honor of the thirteen original colonies.

The American flag is so special that there is a holiday in honor of it. A schoolteacher named BJ Cigrand wanted a day for students to observe the birthday of the flag. On June 14 in 1885, he planned the first birthday celebration for the flag. The idea caught on with other teachers and kids, and after many years, Flag Day became a holiday!

1. Why did the United States need a new flag?

a) George Washington didn't like the design of the British flag.

b) America was gaining freedom from England and needed its own flag.

c) There were thirteen new colonies.

2. What do the stripes on the flag represent?

a) The thirteen stripes represent the thirteen original colonies.

b) The thirteen stripes represent the United States Continental Congress.

c) There are fifty stripes on the flag to represent the fifty states.

3. How did Flag Day become a holiday?

a) The Continental Congress declared Flag Day a holiday in 1777.

b) People started celebrating Flag Day when Hawaii became a state in 1959.

c) In 1885, a schoolteacher named BJ Cigrand and his students celebrated the flag's birthday.

4. Put these events in order by numbering them from 1 to 4.

a) ___ The Continental Congress agreed on the official design of the flag.

b) ___ Hawaii became a state and another star was added to the flag.

c) ___ George Washington decided that the United States needed its own flag.

d) ___ BJ Cigrand and his students celebrated the first "Flag Birthday."

RECORDING RAINFALL

A **biome** is a community of plants and animals. Each of the biomes listed below has a different climate. This graph shows the average inches of rain each of these biomes receives in a year.

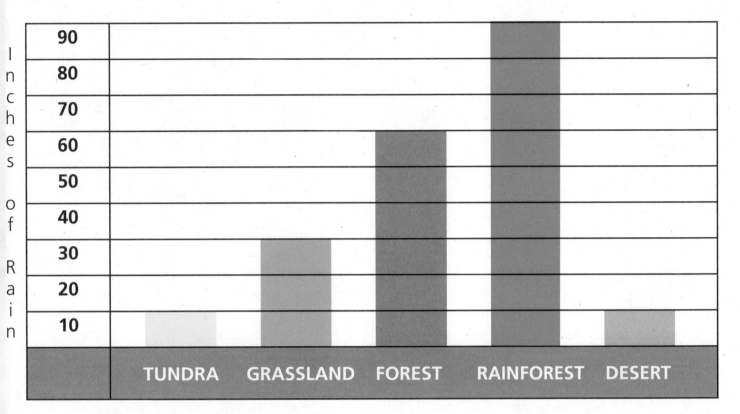

Inches of Rain

| | TUNDRA | GRASSLAND | FOREST | RAINFOREST | DESERT |

90
80
70
60
50
40
30
20
10

Write **true** or **false** for each statement below.

1. A tundra receives more rain than a desert.   _false_

2. A rainforest receives the most rain.   _____

3. A tundra and a grassland receive about the same amount of rainfall.   _____

4. A forest receives about twice as much rain as a grassland.   _____

5. There is no rainfall in a desert.   _____

6. A tundra and a desert receive the least amount of rainfall.   _____

ON YOUR OWN
You can measure the amount of rainfall where you live! Wait for a rainy day, then set up a can outside to collect the rain water. When the rain stops, use a ruler to measure how many inches of rain fell into the can.

A WALK DOWN WORD LANE

A **synonym** is a word that means the same thing as another word. Match each word with its synonym.

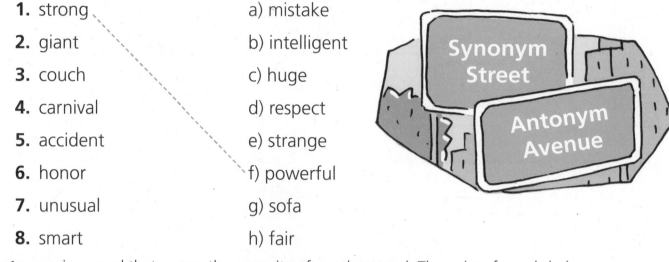

1. strong   a) mistake

2. giant   b) intelligent

3. couch   c) huge

4. carnival   d) respect

5. accident   e) strange

6. honor   f) powerful

7. unusual   g) sofa

8. smart   h) fair

An **antonym** is a word that means the opposite of another word. The pairs of words below are antonyms. Find the pair of words that completes each sentence and write the correct word in each blank.

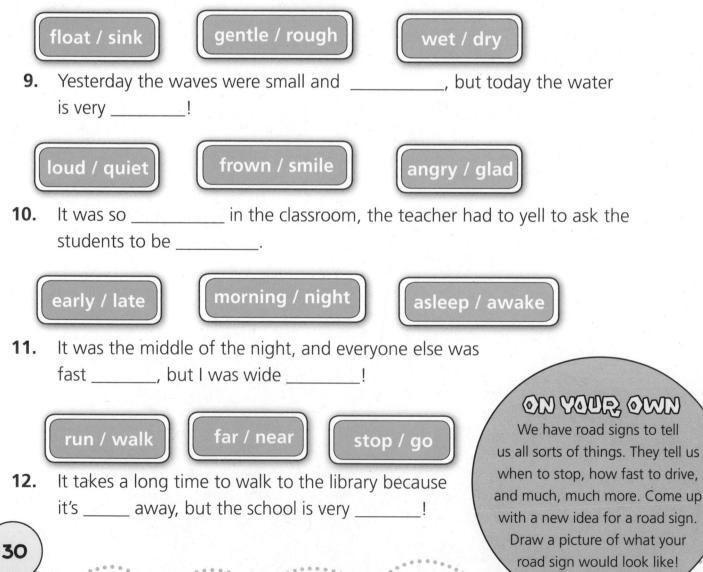

| float / sink | gentle / rough | wet / dry |

9. Yesterday the waves were small and _____, but today the water is very _____!

| loud / quiet | frown / smile | angry / glad |

10. It was so _____ in the classroom, the teacher had to yell to ask the students to be _____.

| early / late | morning / night | asleep / awake |

11. It was the middle of the night, and everyone else was fast _____, but I was wide _____!

| run / walk | far / near | stop / go |

12. It takes a long time to walk to the library because it's _____ away, but the school is very _____!

ON YOUR OWN
We have road signs to tell us all sorts of things. They tell us when to stop, how fast to drive, and much, much more. Come up with a new idea for a road sign. Draw a picture of what your road sign would look like!

CAMP COMMA

Read the passage below. Insert commas where they are needed.

Use commas to separate:
The day, month, and year: *Wednesday, June 21, 1995*
The city and state: *Chicago, Illinois*
Items in a list: *apples, oranges, and berries*

If you want to have a great summer, spend a week at our camp in Portland Oregon. The first day of camp this year is Saturday June 30. Camp runs all summer until Wednesday August 15.

People have been coming to Camp Comma for years! A small campground was opened here on June 1 1955. People came to enjoy the hiking waterfalls and fishing. Then, on April 20 1980, Carl Comma decided to open a camp for kids. Now kids come from all over the country to enjoy Camp Comma. We have kids from San Diego California, and even Fairbanks Alaska.

When you come to Camp Comma, don't forget to bring a sleeping bag a flashlight and a bathing suit.

The deadline to enroll for camp is Friday April 26. Don't wait!

ON YOUR OWN
Write a letter or postcard to a friend. Tell your friend what you've been doing this summer. Be sure to put commas in the correct places in the address!

31

TRIANGLE TRAIL

Follow the trail of triangles. Label each triangle **equilateral**, **isosceles**, or **scalene**. Finish the trail by drawing some of your own triangles and labeling each one!

1.

START

equilateral

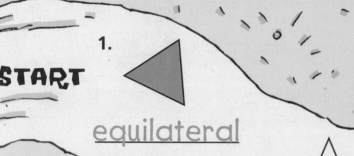

An **equilateral** triangle has all sides of the same length.

An **isosceles** triangle has two sides of the same length.

A **scalene** triangle has no sides of the same length.

2. _____

5. _____

4. _____

3. _____

6. _____

7. _____

8. _____

ON YOUR OWN

Go on a triangle hunt in your own neighborhood! As you walk around, look for different triangle shapes. Figure out if each one is equilateral, isosceles, or scalene.

9. _____

10. _____

FINISH

SHIP SHAPE

Write the name of each four-sided shape.

A **rhombus** has four parallel sides of equal length.

A **parallelogram** has four sides, and opposite sides are parallel.

A **rectangle** has four right angles.

A **square** has four right angles, and all sides are the same length.

1. _____

rectangle

2. _____

3. _____

4. _____

5. _____

6. _____

FAST FACT

Any shape with four sides and four angles is called a **quadrilateral**. In fact, *quad* means four. Look in a dictionary to find other words that use quad in them.

WHAT'S IN A NAME?

Many of our states' names come from Native American words. Match each state with its Native American origin. Look for words that sound similar to the name of the state, then write the matching letter next to each state.

1. Texas _____

2. Tennessee _____

3. Mississippi _____

4. Indiana _____

5. Hawaii _____

6. Illinois _____

7. Alabama _____

8. Alaska _____

a) Named after *Tanasia*, a Cherokee village.

b) From the word *Hawaiki*, which means homeland.

c) Called *Land of the Indians*.

d) From the word *alakshak*, which means great lands.

e) Named after a tribe called the *Alibamu*.

f) From the word *iliniwek*, which means warriors.

g) From the word *messipi*, which means great river.

h) From the word *tejas,* which means allies.

ON YOUR OWN
You can find out the origin and meaning of your own state's name! Go to the library and look up your state in the encyclopedia.

MOON MYSTERIES

The shape of the Moon looks a little different each night. That's because the Moon is moving in an orbit around Earth. We see the Moon from different angles as it reflects light from the Sun. The Moon passes through four main shapes, called the **phases of the Moon**.

FAST FACT
The Moon takes 28 days to orbit around Earth. As it orbits, it keeps the same side facing Earth, so we always see the same side of the Moon. We can never see the back of the Moon from Earth!

Read the description for each phase of the Moon.
Draw a line to match each description with the correct picture.

1. The Moon, Earth, and Sun are in a straight line, but the lighted side of the Moon faces away from Earth. So, the Moon we see looks very dark.

2. The left half of the Moon is still dark, but the right half is lighted. The lighted part gets larger and larger each day.

3. Earth, the Sun, and the Moon are in a straight line, and the lighted side is facing Earth. The Moon is a very bright full circle.

4. The left half of the Moon stays bright, but the right side is dark. The dark part of the Moon grows larger every day.

a) Last Quarter

b) Full Moon

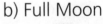

c) New Moon

d) First Quarter

PICNIC OF PLURALS

Write the plural form of each word you see at the picnic.

ON YOUR OWN

Pack a picnic for yourself and enjoy a meal outdoors. Sandwiches, fruit, chips, and canned drinks are great for picnic lunches. Don't forget to throw all your trash away when you're done eating!

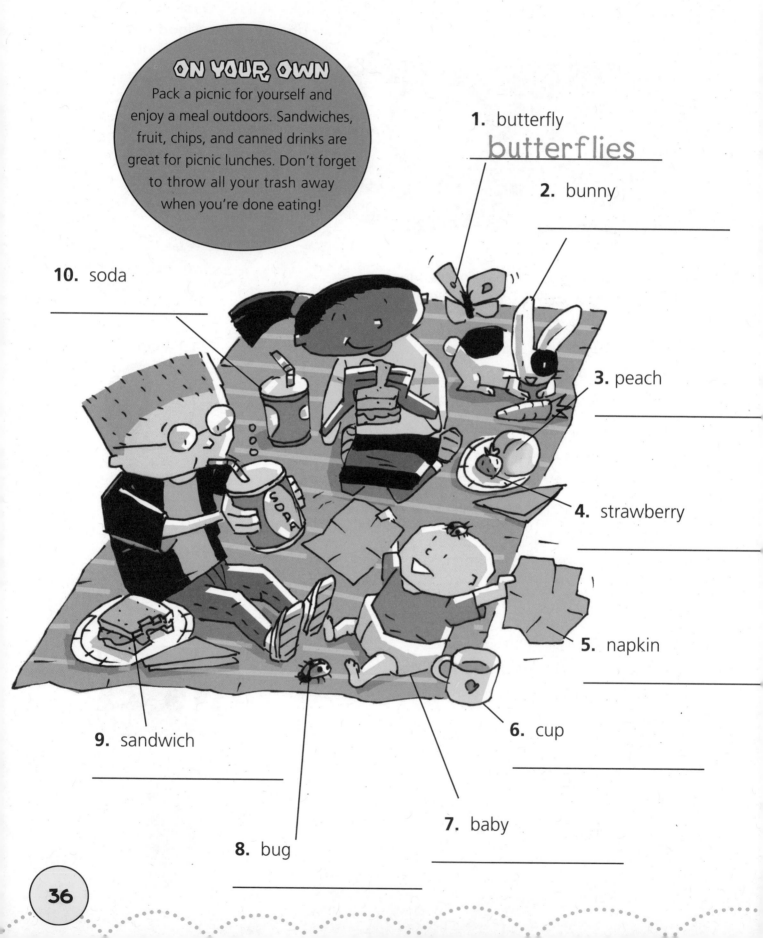

1. butterfly
butterflies

2. bunny
_____

3. peach
_____

4. strawberry
_____

5. napkin
_____

6. cup
_____

7. baby
_____

8. bug
_____

9. sandwich
_____

10. soda
_____

FRAN AND JAN

Read the story. Then answer the questions.

Fran and Jan were twin sisters, so they looked the same. But they couldn't have been more different! Fran liked hiking outdoors and playing sports. Jan liked reading books and writing stories. When the family had to decide where to go on summer vacation, Fran and Jan disagreed.

"Let's go camping and hike to the top of a mountain!" said Fran.

"No way!" said Jan. "I want to read a book by the pool and go to museums."

Fran and Jan's parents suggested lots of vacation spots, but the girls just couldn't agree.

"Since you can't agree," said Fran's mother, "then we'll just have to split up!"

They decided that Fran and her mother would go camping in the mountains. Jan and her father would stay in a beach house.

For the first few days the girls had fun, but soon they started to miss each other. It wasn't really a family vacation if the whole family wasn't together! The family members decided that next year they would find a vacation spot that everyone would enjoy.

1. Why couldn't Fran and Jan agree on a place for the family vacation?

   a) Fran wanted to go somewhere far away, but Jan wanted to stay close to home.

   b) The sisters had different ideas about what they wanted to do.

   c) They didn't want to go anywhere together.

2. Why did Fran's mother decide they should split up?

   a) Fran's parents wanted to do different things.

   b) Fran and Jan didn't want to spend time together.

   c) Fran and Jan couldn't agree on where to go.

3. How did the girls feel after they split up for the vacation?

   a) They were glad that they got to do what they wanted.

   b) They missed each other and felt lonely.

   c) They were angry at their parents.

4. Write some words that describe Fran:

   _____

5. Write some words that describe Jan:

   _____

6. Where do you think the family should go on vacation next year?

   _____

FAST FACT

There are a lot of great national parks across the country. These parks are favorite vacation spots for many Americans. In fact, 65 million Americans visit a national park every year!

THE RIGHT KITE

A **right** angle is a 90 degree angle.
A right angle makes the shape of an **L**.

An angle greater than 90 degrees is called **obtuse**.

An angle less than 90 degrees is called **acute**.

Label each angle **right**, **obtuse**, or **acute**.

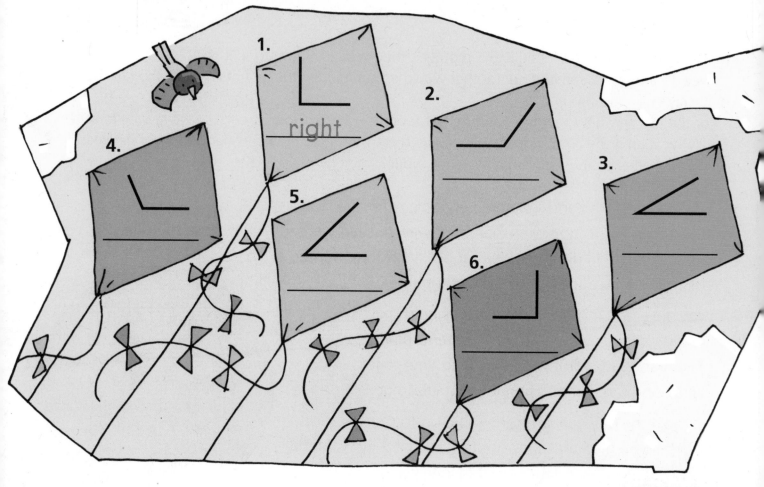

1. right

7. Which drawing has the most right angles?

a)

b)

c)

ON YOUR OWN
Go on a hunt for right angles in your own house. See how many you can find in each room. Find the room in your house that has the most right angles.

38

SHAPES WITH FACES

Three-dimensional shapes have sides and edges.
These sides are called **faces**. Some faces are flat and some are curved.
Count the number of faces on each shape and fill in the chart below.

SHAPES	FLAT FACES	CURVED FACES
1. cube 	6	0
2. pyramid 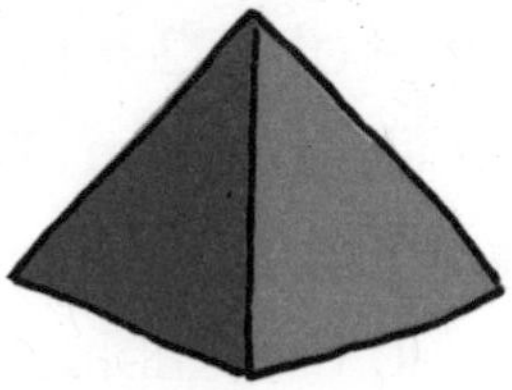		
3. prism 		
4. cone 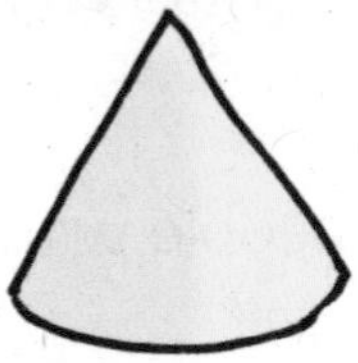		
5. cylinder 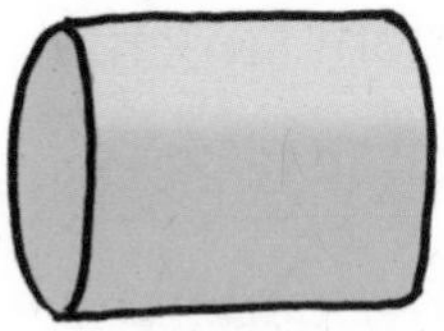		
6. sphere 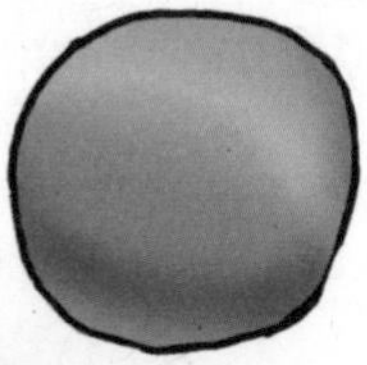		

FUN FACT

Three-dimensional shapes can have lots of faces. A **dodecahedron** is a shape with 12 faces, and an **icosahedron** is a shape with 20 faces!

THE PRESIDENT'S PALACE

Read the story and answer the questions.

Most people know that the White House is the place where the president of the United States lives. It's much more than just a home, however. It's also a workplace, a historical landmark, and an important American symbol.

George Washington had someone begin building what he called the President's Palace in 1792. It wasn't finished until 1800, so George Washington never actually lived in the White House! John Adams was the first president to live there. People nicknamed the house the White House because of its color, but it wasn't until 1901 that Theodore Roosevelt officially named it the White House.

The White House is a busy place and has different rooms for everything that goes on there. In fact, there are six floors in all, with a total of 132 rooms and 32 bathrooms! Only two floors are used for the president and his family to live in. The Oval Office is the president's office. He signs important documents, meets with small groups of people, and makes telephone calls from the Oval Office. In the Cabinet Room, the president sits around a large table for debate and discussion with his staff. The Blue Room is a small room for greeting guests. The State Dining Room is a large room where 140 people can sit down to dinner.

People come from all over to visit the White House and tour some of the rooms. In fact, there are about 6,000 visitors a day!

ON YOUR OWN
Notice how each room in your own house is different. Look at the colors and decorations and think about the purpose of each room. Then come up with a creative name for each room!

Draw a line to match each word with its meaning.

1. cabinet
2. landmark
3. debate
4. documents

a) discussion between people with different opinions
b) important papers
c) a group of people chosen by a political leader
d) a historically important structure

Decide which room in the White House would be the best place for each event.

5. The president is sitting at his desk signing some papers.

_____

6. The president is discussing important issues with many members of his staff.

_____

7. Leaders from another country are coming to a dinner at the White House.

_____

8. A few visitors are coming to meet with the president on a social visit.

_____

POSTCARD FROM ANOTHER PLANET!

Read about Venus and think about how this planet compares to Earth. Then pretend that you're visiting Venus, and write a postcard home to tell your family about it.

VENUS:

- Venus is sometimes called Earth's "twin." That's because Venus is Earth's closest neighbor, even though it is about 25 million miles away.

- The surface of Venus is covered with craters, mountains, volcanoes, and lava plains. There are no oceans on Venus.

- Venus is about 67 million miles away from the Sun. The temperature on Venus is about 900 degrees! In fact, it's the hottest place in the solar system after the Sun.

- The highest point on Venus is Maxwell Montes. It's 7 miles high!

- Venus spins in the opposite direction of Earth. So the Sun rises in the west and sets in the east.

- Venus is surrounded by thick clouds that reflect the Sun's light. This makes Venus the brightest object in the sky after the Sun and the Moon.

FUN FACT

The planet Venus was named after the Roman goddess of love and beauty. Ancient astronomers called it the jewel of the sky.

Dear Family,

I'm having a great time on Venus! So far I've seen _____
_____ .

I like Venus because _____ .
Venus is a lot like Earth because _____
_____ .

Venus is also different from Earth because _____
_____ .

I want to see _____ before I come home!

Sincerely,

_____

LET'S ALL AGREE!

Read each sentence. Underline the subject and circle the verb. If the subject and verb don't agree, rewrite the sentence below. Can the kids agree on what type of pizza to order?

1. Tim and Bill likes lots of cheese.

2. Sally wants pepperoni and mushrooms.

3. Everyone get his or her own drink.

4. The waiter bring a big salad for everyone to share.

5. Bill want mushrooms on the pizza.

6. Tim and Sally get onions instead of mushrooms.

7. All the kids wants pepperoni.

8. Tim, Bill, and Sally order a pepperoni pizza with extra cheese.

FAST FACT

In America, pepperoni is the most popular pizza topping. In other countries, people put all kinds of toppings on pizza. In Japan, you can get squid on your pizza. In Europe, tuna fish is a popular topping!

There are five incorrect sentences. Rewrite each sentence so the subject and verb agree.

_____

_____

_____

_____

_____

LOST LUGGAGE

Erica can't find her luggage at the airport! Read the conversation between Erica and her Aunt Mary. Circle the correct word for each sentence.

Aunt Mary: I can't believe **your / (you're)** finally here!
1

Erica: I can't wait to go to **your / you're** house and see my cousins.
2

Aunt Mary: Yes, **their / they're** very excited to see you!
3

Erica: I need to get my luggage. It should be over **there / their**.
4

Aunt Mary: Do you see **your / you're** bag yet?
5

Erica: **There / They're** it is!
6

Aunt Mary: Wait! That couple is going toward the bag. **Their / They're** picking it up!
7

Erica: It must be **there / their** bag.
8

Aunt Mary: Then where is **your / you're** bag?
9

Erica: **There / Their** it is!
10

Aunt Mary: Hey, here comes that couple. **Their / They're** walking right toward us.
11

Man: Excuse me, is this **your / you're** bag?
12

Erica: Yes! Thank you for bringing it to us. **Your / You're** very kind.
13

Woman: We made a mistake. I hope **you're / your** not too upset.
14

Aunt Mary: Erica, if they had **your / you're** bag, you must have **they're / their** bag!
15   16

Erica: Oops!

ON YOUR OWN

Make luggage tags so your bags don't get lost! Write your name, address, and telephone number on a piece of cardboard. Punch a hole in the cardboard and tie it to your luggage handle with some string.

REGROUP AND RENAME RACE!

Use regrouping and renaming to solve the problems. Find each answer inside the race track and mark it with an **X**. Which race car wins?

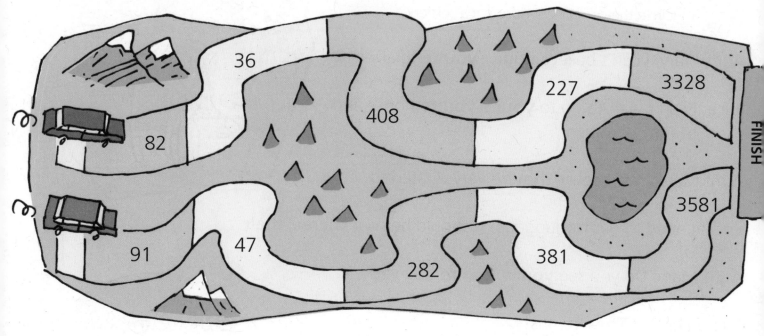

1. 53
   + 29

2. 64
   - 28

3. 76
   + 15

4. 85
   - 38

5. 235
   + 47

6. 433
   - 25

7. 142
   + 239

8. 446
   - 219

9. 1342
   + 2239

10. 5670
   - 2342

FAST FACT
The first car race in the United States was in Chicago, Illinois, in 1895. The course was about 54 miles long, and it took the winning driver 10 hours and 23 minutes to finish!

44

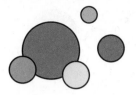

SUMMER SPREE!
Complete each problem. Show your work.

$5.25

$8.50

$3.00

$4.75

$2.50

1. Jane bought 3 beach chairs. What was the total price?

$8.50 + $8.50 + $8.50 = $25.50

2. Kirk bought 4 beach towels. How much did he spend in all?

_____

3. Lucy spent $10.00 on sandals. How many pairs did she buy?

_____

4. Greg has $9.00 he wants to spend on beach balls. How many can he buy?

_____

5. Troy spent exactly $10.00 and he bought 2 items. Which 2 things did he buy?

_____

6. Martha bought a hat and a pair of sandals. How much did she spend in all?

_____

BEN FRANKLIN

Read about the life of Ben Franklin. Then fill in the missing words and dates on the timeline below.

Ben Franklin was a leader in almost every part of American life. Born in 1706 in Boston, Ben loved reading and writing even as a young boy. He wanted everyone to enjoy books, so he started the first public library in 1731. Ben was always thinking of new ideas to help people. In 1744 he invented a heater called the Franklin Stove. This worked much better than a fireplace because all the heat didn't escape through the chimney!

Franklin was a leader in education, and in 1751 he helped start the Philadelphia Academy. This academy later became the University of Pennsylvania. Ben Franklin also played an important role in American politics. He signed the Declaration of Independence in 1776 and helped America become a free country. Ben Franklin is remembered as an American hero!

• TIMELINE •				
1706	_____	_____	_____	_____
Ben Franklin was born in _____ .	Started the first public _____ .	Invented the _____ Stove.	Helped start the _____ Academy.	Signed the _____ of _____ .

FAST FACT

Ben Franklin came up with the idea of Daylight Savings Time! He suggested changing the time with the seasons so people could have more hours of sunlight. That way, people wouldn't have to use so much fuel for lamps.

EXPERIMENT TIME!

This graph shows the results of an experiment that was done with two plants. Read about the experiment and study the graph.

Procedure: Two plastic cups were filled with cotton and five wheat seeds. Cup A had no salt. In Cup B, some salt was added to the bottom of the cup. Both cups were kept moist with water and received plenty of light.

Observations:

	Cup A No Salt	**Cup B** Salt Added
Day 1:	The beans are swelling.	The beans look the same.
Day 2:	Two beans have sprouted.	There is no change.
Day 3:	The other three beans sprouted.	There is slight swelling in two beans.
Day 4:	Stalks are growing from three beans.	Two beans have small sprouts.
Day 5:	Stalks are growing from all five beans.	A total of three beans total have small sprouts. No stalks are growing.

Evidence is an outward fact or sign. An **opinion** is a personal belief or view. Read the sentences below. If the statement is a piece of evidence, write **E**. If the statement is an opinion, write **O**.

1. The beans in Cup A sprouted more quickly than those in Cup B. _____E_____

2. The stalks that grew in Cup A were pretty. _____

3. The beans in Cup A grew stalks within a few days. _____

4. The cups were too small to hold all the beans. _____

5. No stalks grew from the beans in Cup B. _____

6. Based on the experiment, which of the following is the most logical conclusion?
   a) Seeds planted in salty soil will grow much more quickly.
   b) Adding salt helps seeds to soak up more water.
   c) Seeds and plants do not grow as well when salt is present.

ON YOUR OWN
You can watch your own seeds grow at home! Fill a plastic cup with cotton balls and place a few beans inside. Water the beans and keep the cotton moist. In a few days, your beans will start to sprout!

STORIES WITH SENSE

Details that appeal to the five senses help make a story more interesting. Read the narrative. Find the details that appeal to each of the five senses and write them on the lines below.

On the Fourth of July, I went with my family to a carnival. As soon as we got there, I could smell hot dogs and hamburgers cooking and sizzling on the grill. I bit into a juicy slice of watermelon and enjoyed the sweet flavor. We walked through a petting zoo, and I ran my fingers through the soft fur of a goat. At night, the fireworks show started. I heard a crackling sound and then a loud boom. I watched as the dark sky exploded with beautiful colors. What a great day!

Smell: _I could smell hot dogs and hamburgers cooking and sizzling on the grill._

Taste: _____

_____

Touch: _____

_____

Sound: _____

_____

Sight: _____

_____

Now think about a place you visited recently. Write your own narrative using sensory details.

I went to _____.

I saw _____.

It smelled like _____.

I touched a _____ and it felt _____

_____

I heard _____.

I ate a _____ and it tasted like _____

_____.

CAPITAL CARNIVAL

Find the words that need to be capitalized in each sentence and write them on the lines.

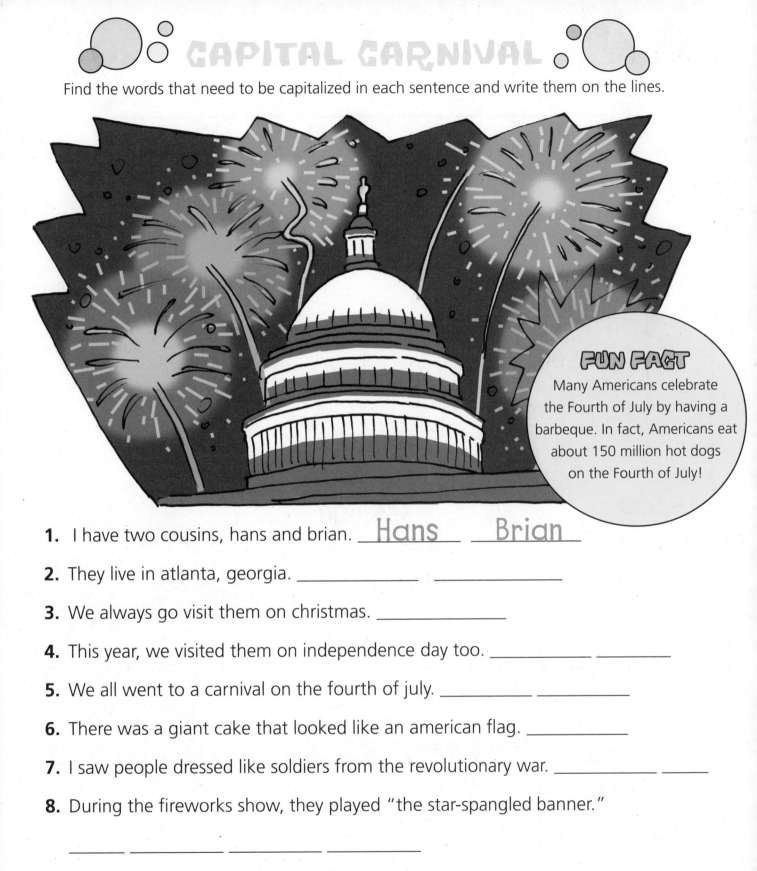

FUN FACT
Many Americans celebrate the Fourth of July by having a barbeque. In fact, Americans eat about 150 million hot dogs on the Fourth of July!

1. I have two cousins, hans and brian. __Hans__ __Brian__

2. They live in atlanta, georgia. _____ _____

3. We always go visit them on christmas. _____

4. This year, we visited them on independence day too. _____ _____

5. We all went to a carnival on the fourth of july. _____ _____

6. There was a giant cake that looked like an american flag. _____

7. I saw people dressed like soldiers from the revolutionary war. _____ ____

8. During the fireworks show, they played "the star-spangled banner."

_____ _____ _____ _____

9. I hear that the best fireworks show is in washington, dc. _____

10. I want to visit my cousins again next july! _____

MAZE OF MILLIONS

Find the maze path that has numbers ordered from smallest to largest.

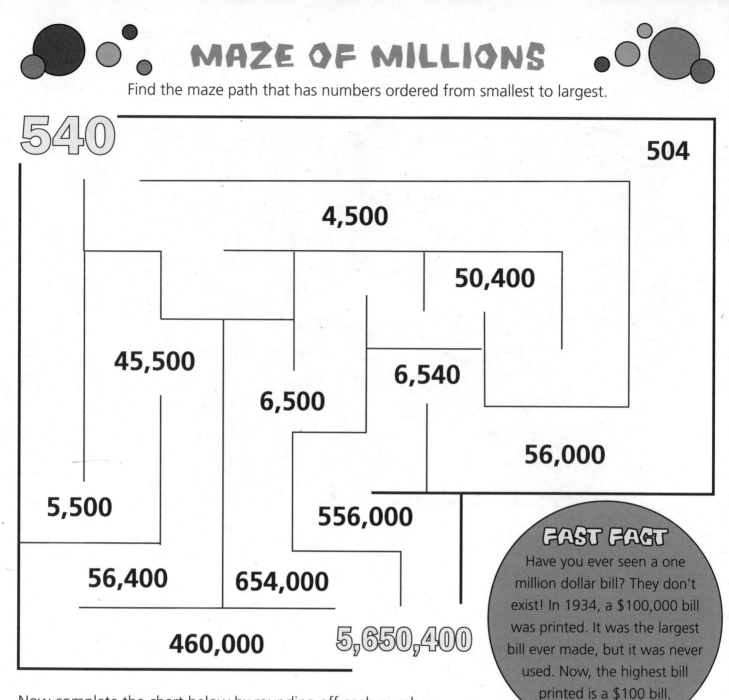

540

504

4,500

50,400

45,500

6,540

6,500

56,000

5,500

556,000

FAST FACT

Have you ever seen a one million dollar bill? They don't exist! In 1934, a $100,000 bill was printed. It was the largest bill ever made, but it was never used. Now, the highest bill printed is a $100 bill.

56,400

654,000

460,000

5,650,400

Now complete the chart below by rounding off each number to the nearest thousand, ten thousand, and hundred thousand.

	THOUSAND	TEN THOUSAND	HUNDRED THOUSAND
385,990	386,000	390,000	400,000
712,183			
149,230			
534,769			

PATTERN PARTY

Fill in the blanks to continue each pattern.

1.

2.

3.

4. 5   10 ___   20 ___   ___   35   ___

5. 4   6   8 ___   12   14 ___   18

6. a   a   b   c   a   a ___ ___ a ___ b ___

ON YOUR OWN
You can make fun patterns with things from around your house. Gather up some forks and spoons from your kitchen and sit down at a large table. Arrange the forks and spoons in a pattern!

MAP RIDDLES

Use the map to solve the riddles. Refer to the compass if you need help.

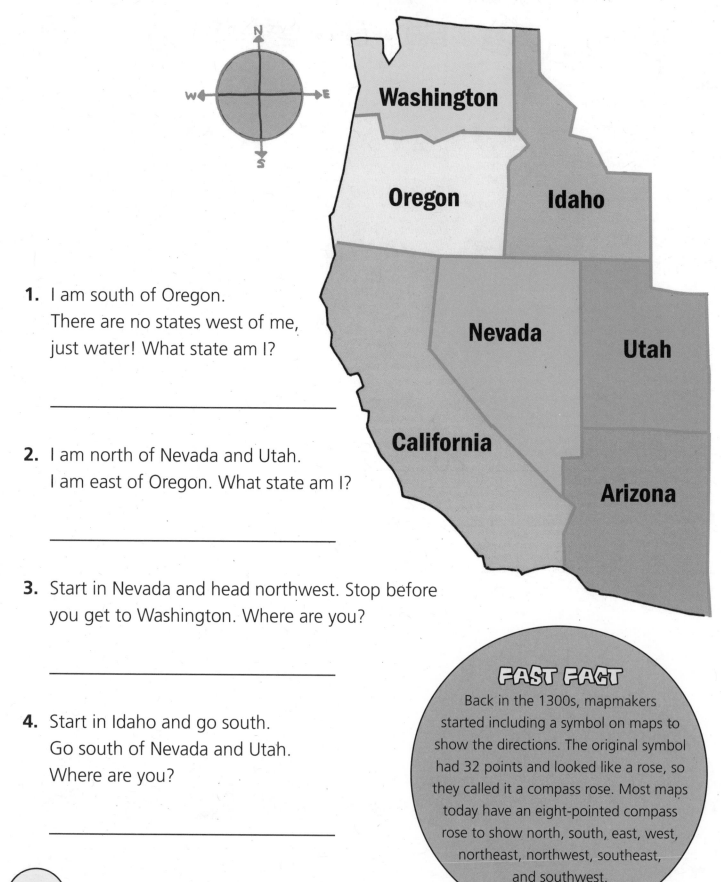

1. I am south of Oregon.
There are no states west of me,
just water! What state am I?

_____

2. I am north of Nevada and Utah.
I am east of Oregon. What state am I?

_____

3. Start in Nevada and head northwest. Stop before
you get to Washington. Where are you?

_____

4. Start in Idaho and go south.
Go south of Nevada and Utah.
Where are you?

_____

FAST FACT

Back in the 1300s, mapmakers
started including a symbol on maps to
show the directions. The original symbol
had 32 points and looked like a rose, so
they called it a compass rose. Most maps
today have an eight-pointed compass
rose to show north, south, east, west,
northeast, northwest, southeast,
and southwest.

ANIMAL APPETITES

This food web shows us what animals eat.

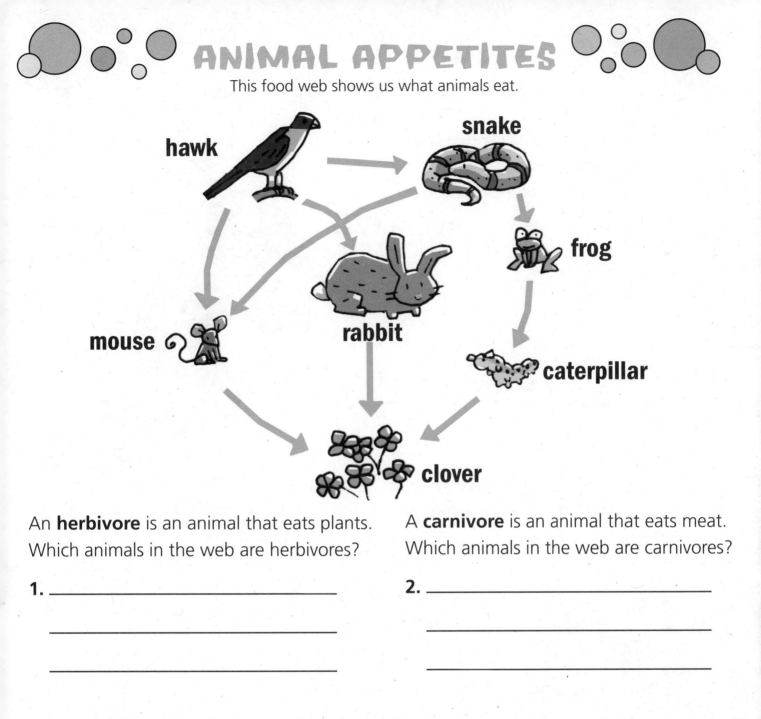

An **herbivore** is an animal that eats plants. Which animals in the web are herbivores?

1. _____

_____

_____

A **carnivore** is an animal that eats meat. Which animals in the web are carnivores?

2. _____

_____

_____

A **predator** is an animal that stalks and eats other animals.

A predator's victim is called **prey**. Use the food web to complete the chart.

Predator	Prey
frog	_____
snake	_____ , _____
_____	rabbit
_____ , _____	mouse

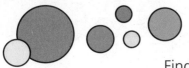

WORD PLAY

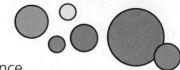

Find the word meaning for the bold word in each sentence.

1. Doug swung at the ball with a **bat**.
   a) a long, wooden club
   b) a small black animal with wings

2. The other team dropped the ball and it started to **roll** away.
   a) a small round piece of bread
   b) to turn over and over

3. The crowd **rose** to its feet and cheered.
   a) to become higher
   b) a flower

4. Doug set a school **record** for the most home runs.
   a) a black thin disc for playing music
   b) the best performance

FAST FACT

How fast does a "fastball" travel? Some pitchers can throw a fastball that goes 90 miles per hour! At that speed, the baseball reaches the batter in less than half a second.

Find the sentence with the same meaning for the bold word.

5. Doug's team was so happy they **beat** the other team.
   a) The chef beat the eggs with a whisk.
   b) My brother can never beat me at checkers.

6. Doug even had a **tear** in his eye!
   a) A big tear rolled down the baby's check.
   b) You should never tear a page out of a book.

COMBINATION VACATION

Read each pair of sentences. Combine the sentences by using commas, adding small words, or leaving words out. Rewrite the new sentence on the line.

1. I went on vacation with my mom and dad. My sister Amy went with us.

_____

2. We drove down the California coast and stopped in three cities. We stopped in San Francisco, Santa Barbara, and San Diego.

_____

_____

3. It was a long drive, so I read a book. I also listened to the radio.

_____

4. In San Francisco we saw the Golden Gate Bridge. We went to a museum, too.

_____

5. I swam in the ocean in Santa Barbara. Amy and Mom swam with me.

_____

6. San Diego was my favorite place. I liked the zoo.

_____

7. We saw monkeys and gorillas. We saw apes, too.

_____

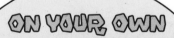

Imagine you could take a road trip anywhere you wanted to go! Decide where you would stop and what you would see on your road trip. Figure out how long it would take to get to each place.

8. Amy liked the tigers the best. I thought the tigers were too scary.

_____

_____

55

FOOD FACTORS

Factors are numbers that you can multiply to equal a product. Factors are always in pairs.

| If you have 12 jellybeans total, you can group them in three different ways. |

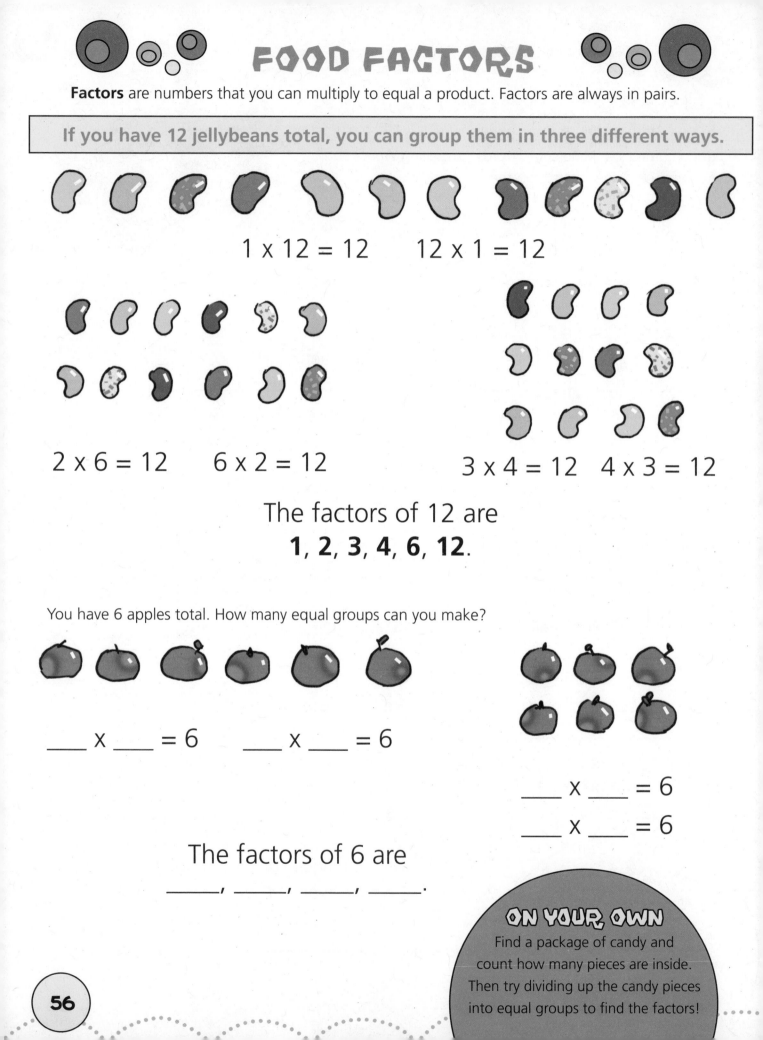

1 x 12 = 12   12 x 1 = 12

2 x 6 = 12   6 x 2 = 12

3 x 4 = 12   4 x 3 = 12

The factors of 12 are
1, 2, 3, 4, 6, 12.

You have 6 apples total. How many equal groups can you make?

___ x ___ = 6   ___ x ___ = 6

___ x ___ = 6
___ x ___ = 6

The factors of 6 are
____, ____, ____, ____.

ON YOUR OWN
Find a package of candy and count how many pieces are inside. Then try dividing up the candy pieces into equal groups to find the factors!

PRIME TIME!

There are 13 prime numbers between 1 and 50. Can you find all 13 inside the TV set? Circle all the prime numbers!

$1 \times 3 = 3 \qquad 3 \times 1 = 1$

The number 3 has only two factors, so it's a prime number.

> A **prime number** is a number that has exactly two factors. The factors are 1 and itself.

17 41 39
33 3
23
47 5 21 29
49
13 19 9
27
37 31
7 11
15

FAST FACT

We have a lot of televisions in America. In fact, 98% of the households in the United States have at least one TV set. More than half of kids under the age of 17 have a TV set in their bedroom.

WHERE IN THE WORLD ARE YOU?

Did you know that for every place on Earth there is a pair of numbers that gives us its location? These numbers are called latitude and longitude. Imaginary lines divide Earth into parts. **Latitude** lines go east and west around the globe. **Longitude** runs north and south. We use a number with a degree symbol and a direction (N, S, E, or W) to name each line. In the middle of Earth, there is a latitude line marked 0°. This line is called the equator. You can find any location on Earth if you know the latitude and longitude!

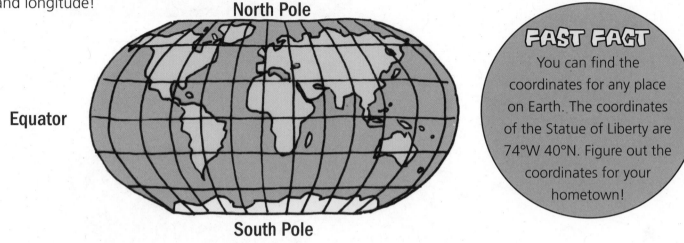

FAST FACT
You can find the coordinates for any place on Earth. The coordinates of the Statue of Liberty are 74°W 40°N. Figure out the coordinates for your hometown!

Find each item on the grid and give the latitude and longitude lines.
Don't forget to watch for the N, S, E, and W marks!

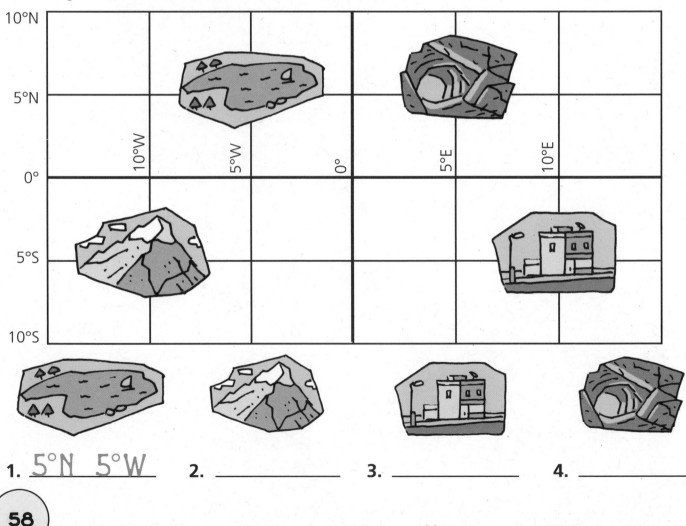

1. 5°N 5°W   2. _____   3. _____   4. _____

ECOSYSTEMS ARE EVERYWHERE

What do a small sand dune and a huge desert have in common? Both are **ecosystems**! An ecosystem is any community of plants and animals and the environment they live in. All of the living things in an ecosystem interact with each other. Here are a few common types of ecosystems:

Forest: Tree-filled woodlands

Coastal: Beaches, oceans, marine areas

ECOSYSTEM

Freshwater: Rivers, streams, and lakes

Urban: Cities and towns filled with people

Grassland: Grassy meadows and prairies where cattle graze

Write the name of the ecosystem that best describes each place.

1. Tide pools _____coastal_____

2. New York City _____

3. A mountainside of pine trees _____

4. Lake Michigan _____

5. A cow pasture _____

6. A coral reef _____

7. A busy street with skyscrapers _____

8. The Mississippi River _____

ON YOUR OWN
You have lots of different ecosystems in the community where you live! See how many different types of ecosystems you can find in your own town. Remember, an ecosystem can be a very small community of living things.

NO ORDINARY ORDER

Read the story. Then number the sentences **1** to **8** to show the correct order of events.

Stacy and Sarah spent all morning rollerblading at the park. Soon, it was lunchtime and the girls were hungry.

"Let's go get a hamburger at the Burger Barn," Stacy suggested.

"That sounds good," said Sarah, "but the Burger Barn is too far to walk."

"It's not too far to rollerblade there," said Stacy.

"Good idea. Let's go!" Sarah said.

The girls rollerbladed to Burger Barn. When they got there, they went to the window and ordered burgers, fries, and soda.

"Let's rollerblade while we wait for our food," said Stacy.

Sarah said, "Okay! It will be fun. I'll race you!"

The girls took off toward the park.

Suddenly, Stacy stopped. "Oh, no," she said. "We forgot to pick up our food! We were so excited about racing to the park, we left our food at the window!"

_____ Stacy suggested that the girls rollerblade while they wait for their food.

_____ The girls took off toward the park.

_____ It was lunchtime and the girls were getting hungry.

_____ They decided to rollerblade to the Burger Barn.

_____ Sarah suggested that the girls race.

___1___ Stacy and Sarah rollerbladed around the park.

_____ They realized that they had left their food at the Burger Barn!

_____ Stacy and Sarah ordered their food.

FAST FACT
Why are hamburgers called hamburgers if they aren't made of ham? The hamburger came to America from Germany, where it was called a Hamburg-style steak.

THE ART OF THE APOSTROPHE

A **contraction** is two words put together to make one. For example, *he will* becomes *he'll*. A **possessive** shows that someone owns the thing that comes after the possessive. For example, *the flowers that belong to Mom* becomes *Mom's flowers*. An **apostrophe** tells whether a word is a contraction or a possessive. Use apostrophes to form new words below.

1. I am

_____I'm_____

2. can not

_____

3. she will

_____

4. does not

_____

5. we are

_____

6. is not

_____

7. she is

_____

8. has not

_____

Use an apostrophe to form the possessive.

9. the shoes that belong to Jim

_____ shoes

10. the box that belongs to Dad

_____ box

ON YOUR OWN

You can make your own watercolor paint at home. Just mix a package of powdered drink mix with a cup of warm water. Then use a paintbrush to create a painting that looks great and smells sweet too!

61

GET INTO SHAPE

The **perimeter** of a shape is the total distance around its sides. To get the perimeter, add all the sides together. The **area** is the amount of space taken up by the entire shape. To get the area, multiply the length by the width. Always write the area with the unit of measurement and the squared sign.

20 yards

10 yards

Perimeter = 20 + 20 + 10 + 10 = 60 yards.

Area = 20 x 10 = 200 yards^2

FUN FACT
A football field is 120 yards long and 53.5 yards wide, including the end zones. This means that the area of a football field is 6,420 square yards, and the perimeter is 347 yards!

Find the perimeter and the area of each shape.

1.

5 cm

3 cm

Perimeter = _____ + _____ + _____ + _____ = _____ cm
Area = _____ x _____ = _____ cm^2

2.

6 inches

5 inches

Perimeter = _____ + _____ + _____ + _____ = _____ in
Area = _____ x _____ = _____ in^2

3.

7 ft

2 ft

Perimeter = _____

Area = _____

4.

4 cm

4 cm

Perimeter = _____

Area = _____

5.

8 in

1 in

Perimeter = _____

Area = _____

MATH MAGIC

Complete the division and multiplication problems.

1. 2435
   x 71

2. 7645
   x 56

3. 9310
   x 13

4. 7628
   x 29

5. 9025
   x 52

6. 5471
   x 34

7. 3)6750

8. 7)6741

9. 5)3490

10. 6)2190

11. 9)5868

12. 2)1270

ON YOUR OWN

Do you know any magic tricks? If so, put on a show for your friends and family. If you do not know any magic tricks, ask a parent to help you find some simple tricks to learn. You could be the next famous magician!

VOTE FOR ME!

Read about how we elect our leaders. Then solve the riddles below!

President

There is only one president at a time. A president serves for four years. A president can be reelected only one time. So, the longest time a president can serve is for eight years total. You must be at least 35 years old to run for president.

Senator

Every state has two senators. Senators serve for six years. You must be at least 30 years old to run for senator.

Representative

The number of representatives is different for each state. The higher the population, the more representatives a state has. There are always 435 representatives total. You must be 25 years old to run. A representative serves for two years.

1. I serve for four years and can be reelected one time. What am I?

   president

2. There are two of me from every state. What am I?

   _____

3. Each state has a different number of me, depending on its population. California has 53 of me. Rhode Island has two. What am I?

   _____

4. There is only one of me at a time! I am always at least 35 years old. What am I?

   _____

5. There are 435 of me total. I serve for two years. What am I?

   _____

6. I serve for six years. I am always at least 30 years old. What am I?

   _____

FAST FACT

In 1940, Franklin D. Roosevelt was the first president elected for a third term. Then he was elected for a fourth term in 1944! After this, the 22nd Amendment was added to the Constitution. This amendment says that presidents can only serve for two terms.

POLLEN POWER

Female plants need to make new seeds, but they can't do it on their own. They need to get a special yellow dust, called pollen, from male plants. This is called **pollination**. The pollen travels from one plant to the next.

Sometimes the wind carries the pollen from one plant to another. Sometimes different insects, such as bees, can carry the pollen. As bees land on flowers to drink their nectar, some of the pollen gets stuck to them. When they fly to the next flower, the pollen falls off. Larger animals, such as hummingbirds, do the same thing. Pollen can also be carried by water.

Pollination can happen a few different ways. What's important is that the pollen gets to the female plant so that new seeds can be made!

1. Name four ways that pollen travels:

wind

_____

_____

_____

ON YOUR OWN
Find a flower that has some pollen, and rub the petals between your fingers. You should see small, bright-colored grains that stick to your fingers. You can see how the pollen gets stuck on insects and animals!

2. Number the sentences **1** through **5** to show the correct order of events.

_____ Some pollen lands on a female plant.

_____ A big gust of wind comes along and carries the pollen with it.

_____ The plant is pollinated, and a new seed is made.

_____ A male plant has a yellow dust called pollen.

_____ The seed is planted and a new plant begins to grow.

DOUBLE BUBBLE

Read both passages. Answer the questions to complete the chart below. Compare the answers for each paragraph.

A.

Modern-day chewing gum was actually invented by accident! A man from Mexico was looking for a substitute for rubber. He asked an inventor named Thomas Adams to experiment with a substance called chicle. The chicle didn't work as a rubber substitute. However, as Adams discovered, it did make a tasty chewing gum!

B.

Betty wanted to make the biggest bubble ever. She put lots of gumballs in her mouth and chewed them up. Then, she blew a giant bubble. Just as she was admiring her bubble, a big gust of wind came along. The bubble popped all over her face!

	Passage A	Passage B
1. Is the passage fiction or nonfiction?	nonfiction	
2. What is the main idea of the passage?		
3. What is a good title for the passage?		

ROLLER COASTER REFERENCES

Complete the chart by writing what type of reference material you would use.
The reference materials are listed for you.

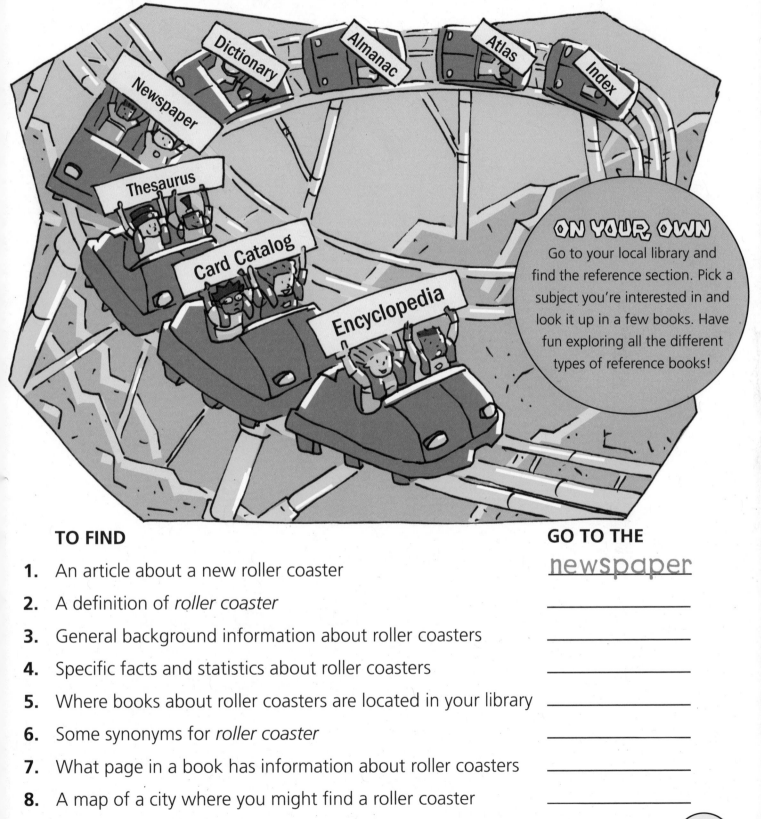

ON YOUR OWN

Go to your local library and find the reference section. Pick a subject you're interested in and look it up in a few books. Have fun exploring all the different types of reference books!

TO FIND	**GO TO THE**
1. An article about a new roller coaster	newspaper
2. A definition of *roller coaster*	_____
3. General background information about roller coasters	_____
4. Specific facts and statistics about roller coasters	_____
5. Where books about roller coasters are located in your library	_____
6. Some synonyms for *roller coaster*	_____
7. What page in a book has information about roller coasters	_____
8. A map of a city where you might find a roller coaster	_____

FUNNY FRACTIONS

If a numerator and denominator in a fraction are the same number, the fraction is equal to 1. If a fraction below is equal to 1, circle the letter. Write all the circled letters in order on the lines below to answer the riddle.

$$\frac{4}{4} = 1$$

What do you call a flying pizza?

A	T	P	O	I	E
$\frac{4}{4}$	$\frac{1}{2}$	$\frac{2}{2}$	$\frac{3}{2}$	$\frac{9}{9}$	$\frac{5}{5}$

I	N	O	T	H	E
$\frac{11}{11}$	$\frac{3}{3}$	$\frac{2}{22}$	$\frac{6}{6}$	$\frac{10}{10}$	$\frac{8}{8}$

I	T	S	K	Y	E
$\frac{6}{9}$	$\frac{11}{1}$	$\frac{7}{7}$	$\frac{1}{1}$	$\frac{12}{12}$	$\frac{7}{1}$

A _____ _____ _____ _____

FRACTION FUN

A **mixed number** is a whole number and a fraction. For example, $1\frac{1}{3}$ is a mixed number. You can change an improper fraction to a mixed number with a proper fraction. Change each improper fraction below into a mixed number with a proper fraction.

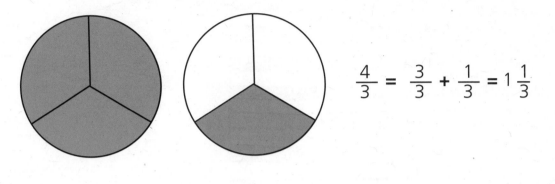

$$\frac{4}{3} = \frac{3}{3} + \frac{1}{3} = 1\frac{1}{3}$$

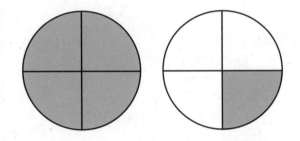 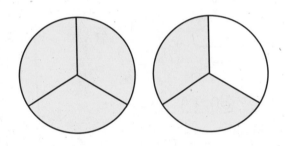

1. $\frac{5}{4} = \frac{4}{4} + \frac{1}{4} = \underline{\hphantom{xxx}}$

2. $\frac{5}{3} = \frac{3}{3} + \frac{2}{3} = \underline{\hphantom{xxx}}$

3. $\frac{7}{5} = \frac{5}{5} + \frac{2}{5} = \underline{\hphantom{xxx}}$

4. $\frac{8}{6} = \frac{6}{6} + \frac{2}{6} = \underline{\hphantom{xxx}}$

5. $\frac{5}{3} = \frac{3}{3} + \underline{\hphantom{xxx}} = \underline{\hphantom{xxx}}$

6. $\frac{3}{2} = \frac{2}{2} + \underline{\hphantom{xxx}} = \underline{\hphantom{xxx}}$

7. $\frac{6}{5} = \underline{\hphantom{xxx}} + \underline{\hphantom{xxx}} = \underline{\hphantom{xxx}}$

8. $\frac{8}{5} = \underline{\hphantom{xxx}} + \underline{\hphantom{xxx}} = \underline{\hphantom{xxx}}$

ON YOUR OWN

Look through a cookbook and find a recipe that uses mixed numbers. Change each mixed number into an improper fraction.

GOVERNOR WORD GUESS

Learn about the job of a governor as you read the passage. Fill in each blank with a word from the word list.

ON YOUR OWN
Find out who the governor is for the state you live in. Visit your state's official website and learn about what your governor is doing in your state!

mansion   budget   educational   vote   taxes   governor   citizens   fifty   constitution   laws

The United States of America is made up of (1) _____fifty_____ different states, and each one is unique! Each state has its own government and even its own (2) _____. The leader of a state is called a (3) _____. A governor is elected by the (4) _____ of the state. So, if you live in New Jersey, you can't (5) _____ for the governor of Colorado. The governor has a very busy job. A governor helps handle the state's money and oversees the (6) _____. He or she has to make sure that the state collects (7) _____. He or she also has to watch over the (8) _____ system and make sure the schools are doing a good job. The governor helps make and pass (9) _____ for the state. This is a tough job and a lot of work, but there is one perk. The governor gets to live in the governor's (10) _____ while he's in office!

ROCK SEARCH

Read about the three different types of rock. Then find each bold word in the word search below.

Igneous Rock

Igneous means made by heat, so it's no wonder that these rocks come from **volcanoes**! Melted rock, called **magma**, pushes through cracks in the Earth's crust. The lava cools and hardens into igneous rock.

FAST FACT
Rocks are used to make all sorts of important things. For example, quartz is used to make watches and clocks!

Metamorphic rock

Metamorphic rock is a rock that has changed. **Heat** and **pressure** change igneous and sedimentary rocks into metamorphic rock. In fact, the word metamorphic means "to **change**."

Sedimentary Rock

Sedimentary rocks are made of many layers. **Layers** of soil, sand, mud, and even seashells squeeze together and harden into rock. We can find **fossils** like dinosaur **bones** buried in sedimentary rock.

```
S  E  D  I  M  E  N  T  A  R  Y
E  V  M  A  E  C  H  P  R  G  E
D  F  A  M  T  A  M  O  R  L  Y
V  O  L  C  A  N  O  E  S  A  B
I  S  A  O  M  A  G  M  A  Y  O
G  S  Y  B  O  N  P  R  E  S  N
F  I  E  P  R  E  S  S  U  R  E
O  L  R  R  P  I  G  N  E  U  S
L  S  S  C  H  E  A  T  L  D  E
I  F  O  C  I  G  N  E  O  U  S
S  E  D  I  C  H  A  N  G  E  I
```

POOL POETRY

A **simile** is a comparison using the words *like* or *as*.
The pool was as big as a lake!

A **metaphor** is when you say that one thing is another thing.
I was a long raft, floating and drifting on the water.

Personification is when you describe objects with human-like feelings or actions.
The hot sun nagged at me to go to the pool.

ON YOUR OWN
Read your favorite story, and look for similes, metaphors, and personification as you read. See how many examples of each you can find in the story!

Read each sentence and decide if it uses a **simile**, **metaphor**, or **personification**.
Check the correct column.

	Simile	Metaphor	Personification
1. It was so hot outside, it felt like an oven.	✓		
2. The cool water called out to me.			
3. I raced toward the water like a cannonball.			
4. The splash I made was as big as a tidal wave.			
5. The water felt like cold ice.			
6. I was a fish, darting through the water.			
7. The water danced around me and tickled my toes.			
8. The divers were graceful swans gliding through the air.			

Now write a few of your own!

Simile: _____

Metaphor: _____

Personification: _____

72

WORD WAGON

As you read the passage, figure out the part of speech for each bold word. Write the words in the correct column below.

During the middle of the nineteenth century, Americans **started** moving west. They hoped to settle down on new land, so they were called **settlers**. The **journey** west was very **challenging**. There weren't any cars, so people rode in covered wagons. **Big** groups of wagons **traveled** together in a wagon train.

The settlers **bravely** faced the 2,000-mile trip west. The wagons could not travel very **quickly**, so the **trip** took about six months. They crossed prairies, deserts, and steep mountains. They even had to ride across flooded rivers. There were so many wagons traveling at the same time, the trail **was** very **dusty**. The settlers **courageously** continued on until they reached the west.

FAST FACT
Covered wagons were strong enough to carry 3,500 pounds. To keep it from sinking in the mud, the wheels were 5 or 6 feet high!

Nouns	Verbs	Adjectives	Adverbs
_____	_____	_____	_____
_____	_____	_____	_____
_____	_____	_____	_____

HOW MUCH DOES JOE OWE?

Joe doesn't have enough money to buy what he wants. He has to borrow money. How much money does he owe? Use the number line to help. Write what Joe owes as a **negative number**, a number that is less than zero.

Joe had 4 dollars. He wanted to buy a hat for 6 dollars
How much does Joe owe?
Joe owes __2__ dollars.
__-2__

-10 -9 -8 -7 -6 -5 -4 -3 -2 -1 0 1 2 3 4 5 6 7 8 9 10

1. Joe had 2 dollars. He wanted to buy a burger for 4 dollars. Joe owes _____ dollars.

_____

2. Joe had 3 dollars. He wanted to buy some shoes for 7 dollars. Joe owes _____ dollars.

_____

3. Joe had 5 dollars. He wanted to buy a shirt for 8 dollars. Joe owes _____ dollars.

_____

4. Joe had 2 dollars. He wanted to buy a game for 6 dollars. Joe owes _____ dollars.

_____

5. Joe had 1 dollar. He wanted to buy a book for 3 dollars. Joe owes _____ dollars.

_____

6. Joe had 4 dollars. He wanted to buy a pizza for 7 dollars. Joe owes _____ dollars.

_____

FAST FACT
Numbers don't have to stop at zero! In fact, we use negative numbers for all kinds of things. For example, we use negative numbers to express temperatures that are below zero.

ROCKIN' ROUND OFF

A **whole number** is a number with no decimals. The numbers **1** and **2** are whole numbers. To round to the nearest whole number, look at the decimal. The number **1.7** would be rounded to **2**. Numbers exactly halfway, like 3.5, should be rounded up. Round each number to the nearest whole number.

| 1 | 1.1 | 1.2 | 1.3 | 1.4 | 1.5 | 1.6 | 1.7 | 1.8 | 1.9 | 2 |

1. 1.2 ___1___

2. 1.9 _____

3. 2.4 _____

4. 3.6 _____

5. 4.1 _____

6. 5.8 _____

7. 3.3 _____

8. 6.1 _____

9. 5.9 _____

10. 4.4 _____

11. 6.7 _____

12. 5.5 _____

ON YOUR OWN
Next time you're at the store, take a look at some of the price tags. Practice rounding off each amount to the nearest dollar. Try rounding off to the nearest ten dollars or hundred dollars too!

Round off to the nearest dollar.

13. $1.89 _____

14. $5.12 _____

15. $10.25 _____

16. $9.09 _____

17. $19.71 _____

18. $100.62 _____

19. $56.82 _____

20. $10.50 _____

21. $96.20 _____

22. $25.75 _____

23. $18.48 _____

24. $86.73 _____

CONSTITUTION COUNTDOWN

Read the passage and fill in the missing dates and words on the timeline.

On July 4 in 1776, the United States declared independence from Great Britain, and a new country was born. After the Revolutionary War was over, Americans needed to decide how they would govern themselves. In 1777, they created the Articles of Confederation. Unfortunately, the Articles of Confederation led to a weak government that needed to be changed.

In May of 1787, delegates from all the states met at a convention in Philadelphia, Pennsylvania. They decided to set aside the Articles of Confederation and write a new Constitution. By September of 1787, the new Constitution was accepted by the delegates. But the delegates then had to convince all the states to vote in favor of it! It wasn't until 1788 that New Hampshire voted to accept the Constitution, and the Articles of Confederation were finally replaced. In 1790, Rhode Island became the last state to vote in favor of the Constitution.

FAST FACT
The U.S. Constitution was written and signed in the same building where the Declaration of Independence was signed. This building is now called Independence Hall.

• TIMELINE •

1776	_____	_____	_____	_____
The United States declared independence from _____ .	The Articles of _____ were created.	In May, delegates met at a convention in _____ _____	The state of _____ _____ voted to accept the Constitution and the _____ of Confederation were replaced.	_____ became the last state to accept the Constitution.

CRYSTAL CAVES

Have you ever seen a crystal vase or glass? You probably noticed that crystal is clear and shiny. It's not at all like a rough, dark rock. And yet, crystals are actually rocks!

Crystals are a type of mineral, and minerals are the building blocks of rocks. A rock is really a big clump of different minerals stuck together. As minerals combine and grow, sometimes they start to change shape. They can develop flat sides with sharp, clear edges. When minerals have lots of space to grow, they form beautiful, large crystals.

Crystals can grow naturally in caves. Some of the largest natural crystals on earth are in a cave in Mexico. The cave is called the Cave of Swords because the crystals look like giant swords. A nearby cave called Cave of Crystals has crystals that are over 20 feet long!

In the left circle, write some facts or words about crystals. In the right circle, write about rocks. In the middle part, write some facts or details that are true for both rocks and crystals.

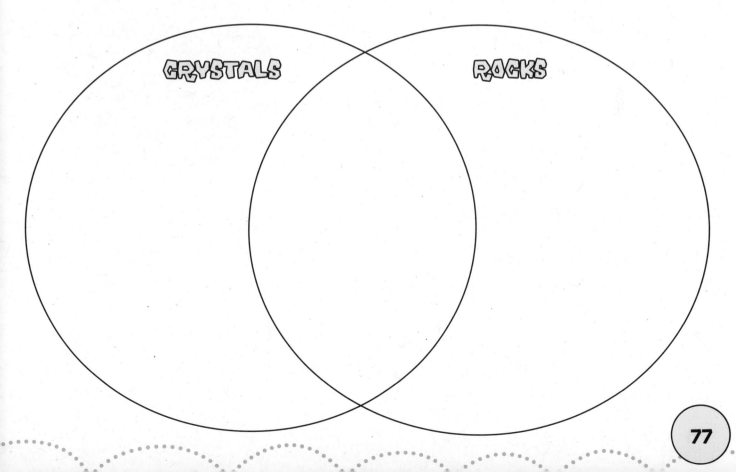

CRYSTALS

ROCKS

HOW TO MAKE A CHOCOLATE SHAKE

Have an adult help you follow the directions to make a delicious chocolate shake!

1. Using an ice cream scooper, put 2 scoops of vanilla ice cream in a blender.

2. Measure 1 cup of milk and add it to the blender.

3. Pour 3 tablespoons of chocolate syrup into the blender.

4. Secure the lid on top of the blender and turn on the power.

5. Blend everything together for ten to fifteen seconds.

6. Pour your milkshake into a glass and enjoy!

WOW!

Fill in the blanks.

Ingredients:

_____ scoops vanilla ice cream

_____ cups milk

_____ tablespoons chocolate syrup

ON YOUR OWN
Practice following directions by cooking something. Choose a simple recipe, and have an adult help you make it.

Read each statement and write **true** or **false**.

1. To follow this recipe you need an ice cream scooper, a blender, and a sharp knife. _false_

2. This recipe calls for chocolate ice cream and milk. _____

3. The recipe tells you to put ice cream in the blender first, then add the milk. _____

4. It is important to turn on the power before securing the lid. _____

5. After blending for ten seconds, you should add the chocolate syrup. _____

6. You should blend everything for ten to fifteen seconds. _____

SPELLING SPEEDWAY

Circle the misspelled words in each lane. The car whose lane has the fewest misspelled words wins the race!

FAST FACT

The most famous speedway in the world is the Daytona International Speedway in Florida, home to a 500-mile race called the Daytona 500. Race cars can go up to 190 miles per hour as they speed around this track!

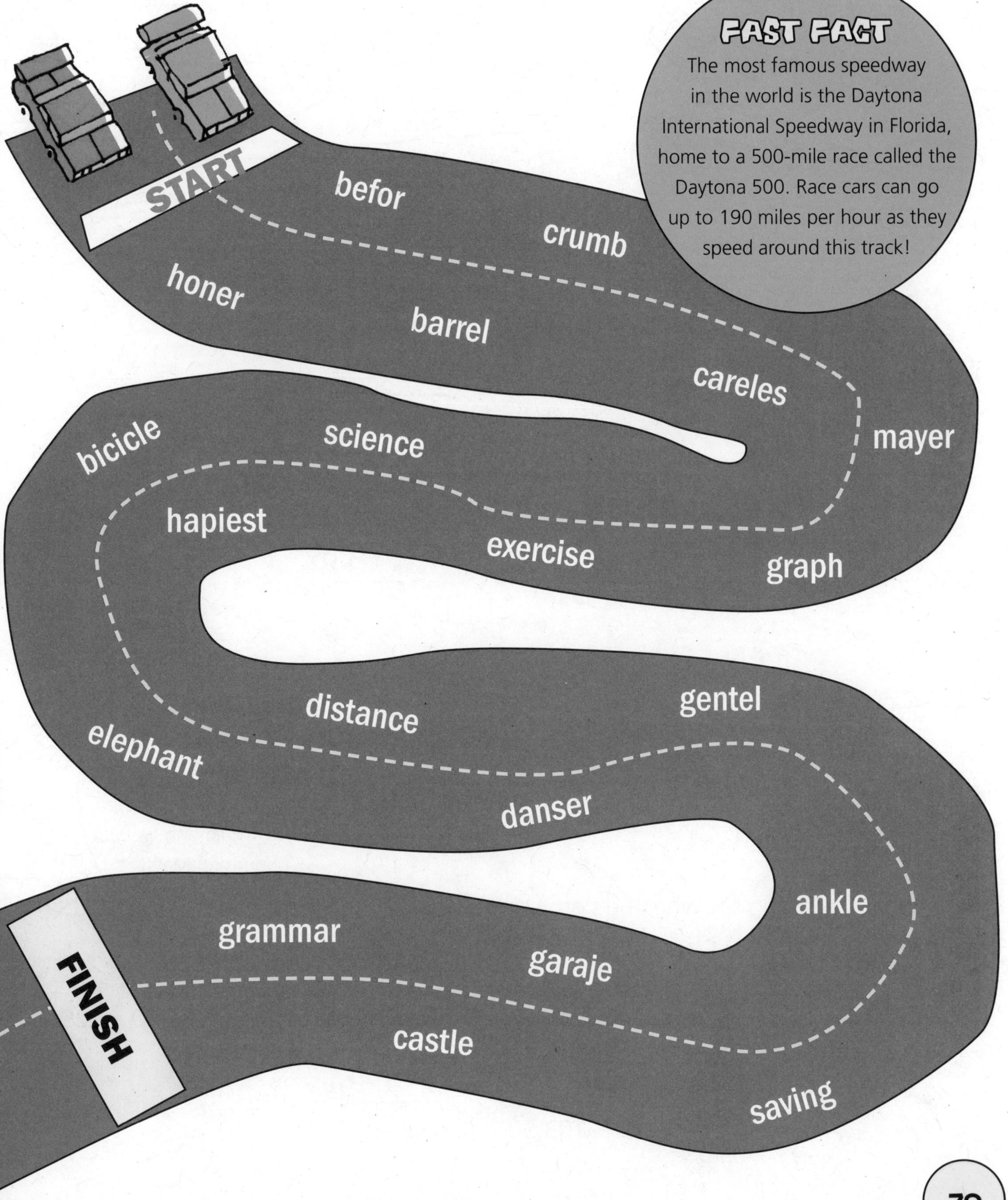

START
befor
crumb
honer
barrel
careles
mayer
bicicle
science
hapiest
exercise
graph
distance
gentel
elephant
danser
ankle
grammar
garaje
castle
saving
FINISH

Multiply to solve each problem. Find the answer below and write the letter.

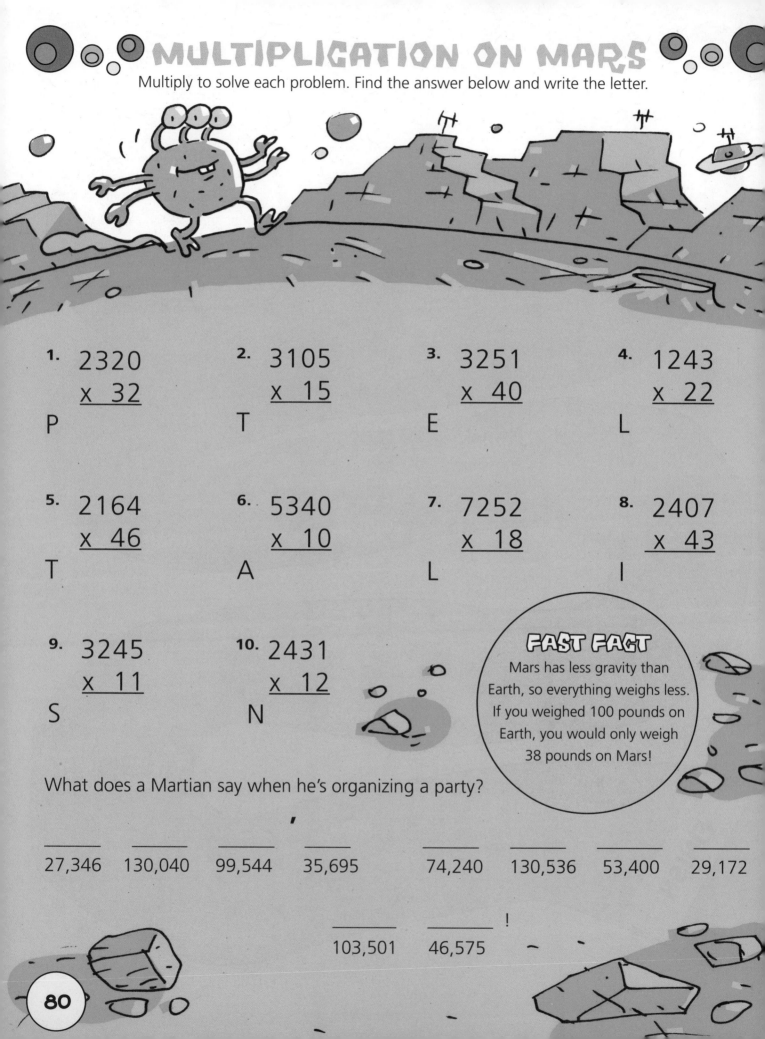

1. 2320
   x 32
   P

2. 3105
   x 15
   T

3. 3251
   x 40
   E

4. 1243
   x 22
   L

5. 2164
   x 46
   T

6. 5340
   x 10
   A

7. 7252
   x 18
   L

8. 2407
   x 43
   I

9. 3245
   x 11
   S

10. 2431
    x 12
    N

FAST FACT

Mars has less gravity than Earth, so everything weighs less. If you weighed 100 pounds on Earth, you would only weigh 38 pounds on Mars!

What does a Martian say when he's organizing a party?

___ ___ ___ ___ '   ___ ___ ___ ___
27,346 130,040 99,544 35,695   74,240 130,536 53,400 29,172

___ ___ ___ ___ !
103,501 46,575

SLIP AND SLIDE DIVIDE

Which slide is faster? Divide to solve each problem. The slide that has the fewest answers with remainders is the faster one!

Slide 1

1. 4)168

2. 5)315

3. 4)133

4. 6)385

5. 7)149

Slide 2

1. 6)252

2. 4)217

3. 2)642

4. 3)263

5. 8)832

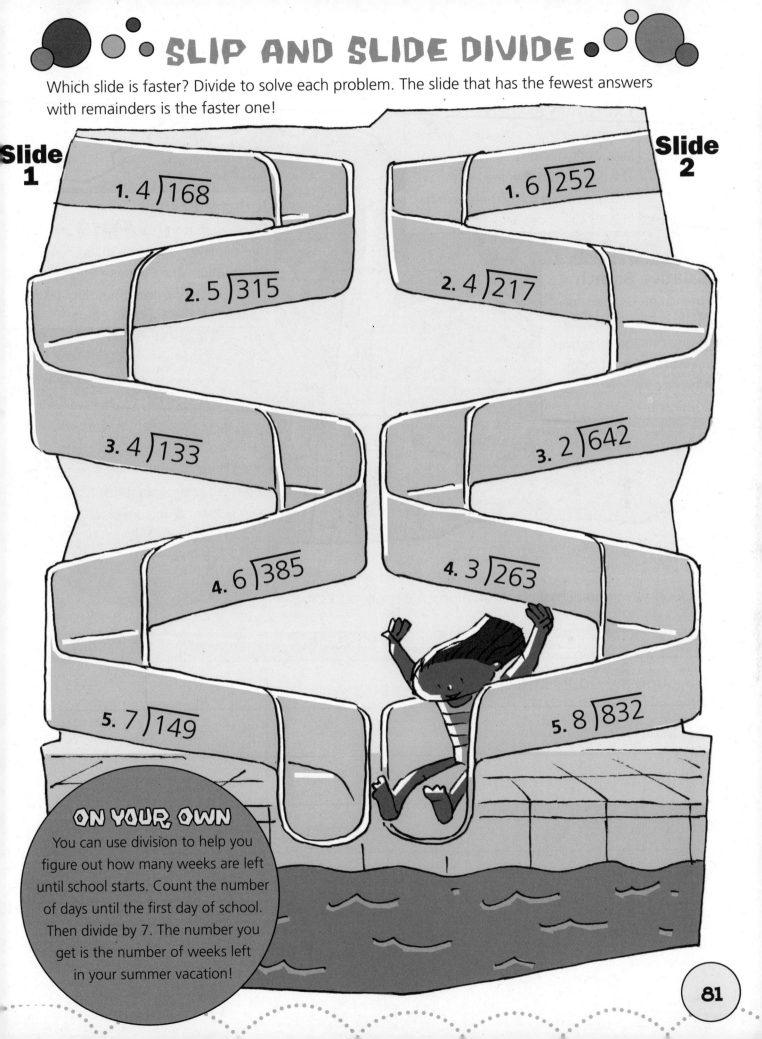

ON YOUR OWN
You can use division to help you figure out how many weeks are left until school starts. Count the number of days until the first day of school. Then divide by 7. The number you get is the number of weeks left in your summer vacation!

BRANCHES OF GOVERNMENT

Executive Branch
This branch makes sure that the laws of the country are obeyed. The president is the head of the Executive branch. The president has helpers called cabinet members.

Legislative Branch
This branch makes laws for the country. The Senate and the House of Representatives are members of this branch. Together, they make up the U.S. Congress.

Judicial Branch
This branch is the court system. It makes sure our laws follow the guidelines in the Constitution. The Supreme Court has nine judges, called Justices. The Chief Justice is the head of the Supreme Court.

FAST FACT
The Founding Fathers wanted to make sure that no one person had too much power, so they spread the power out among the three branches. This way, leaders could check up on one another. This is called a system of **checks and balances**.

Check off which branch of government each person works for.

	Executive	Legislative	Judicial
1. A Supreme Court Justice			✓
2. A senator			
3. A member of the president's cabinet			
4. The Chief Justice			
5. A member of Congress			
6. The president			

WHAT ON EARTH HAPPENED?

Our Earth is constantly changing! Sometimes these changes happen very quickly, like during an avalanche or flood. But usually these changes happen so slowly that we don't even realize it. It all starts when rocks get worn down from rain, ice, or heat. After the rocks crumble, the particles are carried away by natural forces. This is called **erosion**. Over time, erosion can flatten mountains or carve out valleys!

Each box shows a different type of erosion. Label the picture with the correct title.

water erosion	coastal erosion
wind erosion	glacial erosion

ON YOUR OWN
Make a small pile of dirt or soil in your backyard. Check on the pile after several days, and you'll notice that particles were carried away, making the pile smaller. That's erosion!

1. Ocean waves and currents sweep away sandy shores.
coastal erosion

2. A giant moving mass of ice can carry rocks and soil away with it.

3. As rain runs downhill, it carries away soil.

4. As the wind whips across the desert, it picks up dirt and sand.

Why the Pine Is Green

Most trees have leaves that turn yellow and fall to the ground during the winter, but the needles of a pine tree stay green all winter long. The people of Asia had a story to explain why the pine needles never die.

According to the myth, a long time ago pine needles did turn yellow and die in the winter. During this time, there was a hunter who liked to walk deep in the woods. One day, the hunter wandered into a place he had never seen before. He was very surprised when he saw seven tiny people. The tiny people explained that they washed in magic water that made them immortal. Because of this water, they could never die.

The Immortal People were glad to see the hunter because they needed some help. One of their people was missing! A large animal had carried the person away. The hunter agreed to help find the missing person. He found the animal and returned the tiny person to safety. The Immortal People wanted to thank the hunter. They promised to bring him the magic water so that he could become immortal too.

The hunter went back to his village and waited. Many days passed. One day, the women in the hunter's village saw the Immortal People walking toward them. They thought the tiny people looked strange because they were so small. The women laughed and laughed at the tiny people.

What do you think happened next? Write your prediction on the lines below.

_____

_____

_____

Here's how the story ends:

The Immortal People did not like to be laughed at. They were very hurt. They decided not to bring the hunter the magic water. Instead, they dumped the water on the ground near some pine trees. So, the pine trees became immortal. This is why pine trees today have green needles that never die. Was your prediction right?

FAST FACT
Pine trees belong to a type of plant called evergreens. All evergreen trees have leaves that don't turn yellow and fall off during winter. They were given the name "evergreens" because their leaves stay green.

1. The word immortal means:

    a) to be very small.

    b) to never die.

    c) to never have winter.

ON YOUR OWN

You can write your own myth! Think of something that happens in nature, then create a question. (For example, *Why does the Moon shine at night*?) Then write a story to explain the answer!

2. Why did the Immortal People want to thank the hunter?

    a) Because he chased away a large animal.

    b) Because he promised to keep their secret.

    c) Because he helped find the missing person.

3. Why did the village women laugh at the Immortal People?

    a) Because they thought the tiny people were funny.

    b) Because they thought the tiny people looked strange.

    c) Because one of the women told a joke.

4. Why did the Immortal People dump the water on the ground?

    a) Because they were angry with the hunter.

    b) Because they were hurt that the women laughed at them.

    c) Because they wanted the pine trees to stay green.

5. The purpose of the myth is:

    a) To explain why pine needles stay green all winter long

    b) To show people why pine trees are important.

    c) To teach people how to water pine trees.

6. Number the sentences 1 through 6 to show the order of events.

    _____The village women laughed at the Immortal People.

    _____The hunter discovered a group of tiny people deep in the woods.

    _____The Immortal People promised they would bring the hunter some magic water.

    _____The hunter helped return the missing person to the group of Immortal People.

    _____The Immortal People dumped the magic water on the ground.

    _____The hunter waited and waited for the Immortal People to bring the water.

HERE COMES THE ICE CREAM TRUCK!

How many times did the ice cream truck stop on each street? Use the data below to fill in the chart. Each truck stands for 2 stops. Then answer the questions below.

Elm Street 🚚🚚

Pinewood Avenue 🚚🚚

Main Street 🚚🚚🚚🚚🚚

Windy Lane 🚚

Cherry Avenue 🚚🚚🚚

10					
8					
6					
4					
2					
0					
	Elm St.	**Main St.**	**Cherry Ave.**	**Pinewood Ave.**	**Windy Ln.**

1. On which street did the ice cream truck make the most stops? _____

2. On which street did the ice cream truck make the fewest stops? _____

3. On which two streets did the ice cream truck make the same number of stops?

   _____ and _____

4. How many more stops did the truck make on Main St. than on Cherry Ave.? _____

5. How many stops total did the truck make on Elm St. and Windy Ln.? _____

6. How many stops did the truck make altogether on all the streets? _____

GRAPH GIGGLES

An **ordered pair** of numbers is used to locate a point. The first number shows how many units across. The second number shows how many units up. Find each ordered pair on the grid and write the letter on the line.

Example: 2, 1

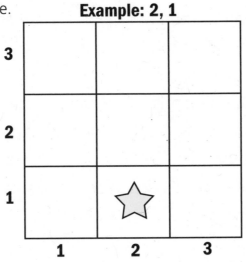

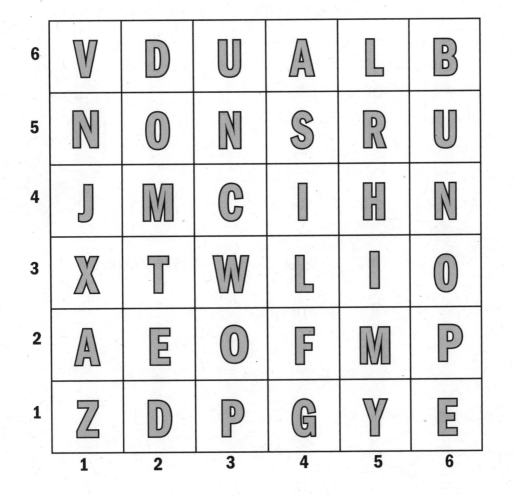

Why was the grid so shy?

Because people were always ____ ____ ____ ____ ____ ____ ____ ____ at him!

(6,2) (3,2) (5,3) (1,5) (2,3) (4,4) (3,5) (4,1)

TWO KINDS OF GOVERNMENT

Read about federal and state governments. Then list which powers each government has in the diagram below.

You may sometimes see two flags flying on a flagpole. These are the American flag and your state flag. That's because both the country and the states have their own governments. Each one has certain powers.

The government for the whole country is called the federal government. Only the federal government has the power to print money. The federal government also handles our country's relationships with other countries. This is called foreign policy. Sometimes, the federal government makes deals, or treaties, with other nations. It also has to protect the country, so it oversees the army and navy. The U.S. Postal Service is run by the federal government, too.

The state government has the power to hold elections for local governments. It gives out licenses for lots of different things—business, driving, marriage, and even fishing! It also votes on whether changes should be made to the Constitution.

Shared powers are things that both federal and state governments do. They both have to collect taxes, build roads, set up courts, and make and enforce laws to protect the health and safety of the people!

FAST FACT
The federal government is the highest authority in the country. That's why the American flag always flies higher than the state flag on a flagpole!

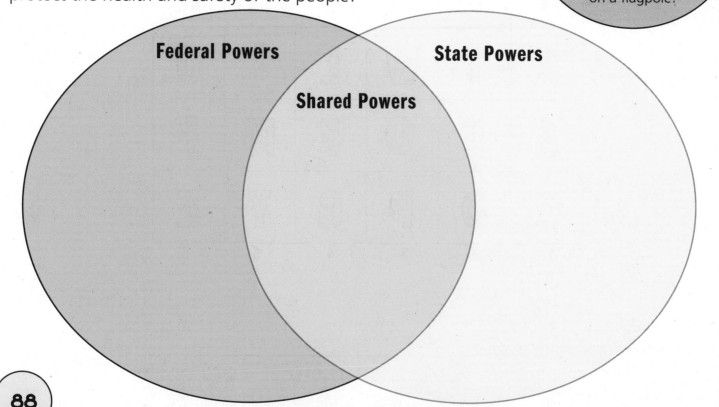

Federal Powers   **State Powers**

Shared Powers

ALL SHOOK UP

Read about earthquakes. Then write **true** or **false** for each statement below.

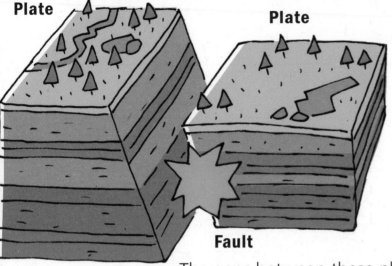

Plate

Plate

Fault

An earthquake is a sudden shaking of the ground. This shaking creates waves of motion called seismic waves. A machine is used to measure seismic waves. This machine is called a seismograph.

What causes an earthquake? The earth's surface is divided into ten large plates and twenty small plates. The gaps between these plates are called faults. Sometimes, these plates move closer together, stretch farther apart, or slip past each other. This causes an earthquake. The point where the plates moved is called the epicenter.

Scientists use a scale called the Richter Scale to express the size, or magnitude, of an earthquake. Earthquakes with a magnitude of less than 2.0 can't be felt by people at all. If the quake reaches a 4.0, it can cause damage. A strong earthquake is 6.0 or above. California is known for having lots of quakes, but the state with the most quakes per year is actually Alaska!

1. Scientists use a seismograph to measure the seismic waves. ___true___

2. Earthquakes happen when plates along the earth's surface suddenly move. _____

3. The Earth has about 500,000 plates. _____

4. Faults are gaps between the Earth's plates. _____

5. The epicenter of an earthquake is the area where the seismograph is. _____

6. An earthquake of 4.0 cannot be felt by people. _____

7. The Richter Scale is used to express the size of an earthquake. _____

8. California has the most earthquakes per year. _____

ON YOUR OWN

You can create your own seismic waves and enjoy a tasty treat! Have your parents help you make a pan of Jell-O. Once the Jell-O is set, tap the side of the pan with a spoon. Watch the Jell-O shake and jiggle, just like the earth's surface does!

BOOK REPORT!

It's time to write your very own book report! First, choose a book that tells a story. After you read it, fill in the information below.

Book title: _____

Author: _____

This book is about _____.

The characters are _____
_____.

The setting of the story is _____.

Here's what happened in the story. First, _____
_____.
Next, _____.
Finally, _____.

My favorite part was when _____
_____
_____.

I liked this book because _____
_____
_____.

FAST FACT
Studies show that kids who read for at least 15 minutes a day will read more than a million words in a year. So keep reading!

PRESIDENT'S PAGE

Choose an American president whom you would like to learn more about. Then go to the library and read about that president in an encyclopedia. Fill in the information below, and you'll have a report!

President's name: _____

During what years did this president serve? _____

Birthplace: _____

Birthdate: _____

When _____ _____ was young, he _____
        first name   last name

_____.

As he got older, he _____

_____.

He became president in _____.

Here are some of the important things he did when he was president:

_____

_____

_____

If I could meet this president, this is what I would ask him:

_____

_____

_____

FAST FACT

We celebrate President's Day to honor two very important presidents: George Washington and Abraham Lincoln. Both men were born in February, so President's Day is celebrated on the third Monday in February.

SUMMER READING LIST

Here are some books for readers going into fourth grade to enjoy during the summer months.

Chocolate Touch by Patrick Skene Catling
In a modern-day twist on the King Midas story, a boy named John Midas turns everything into chocolate when it touches his lips.

Muggie Maggie by Beverly Cleary
Maggie's cursive is so sloppy that her name looks like "Muggie." When Maggie refuses to learn cursive, her teacher comes up with a plan to help.

James and the Giant Peach by Roald Dahl
James befriends a band of garden insects and goes on exciting adventures, all while being inside a giant peach the size of a house.

Matilda by Roald Dahl
Matilda is an exceptionally smart young girl whose parents are too busy watching television to notice her many talents. In this book she uses her wits to outsmart her evil headmistress and ensure her favorite teacher's financial security.

The Black Stallion by Walter Farley
This book series follows the adventures of a boy and his horse who survive on an island after being shipwrecked.

Jim Ugly by Sid Fleischman
Twelve-year-old Jake goes on a wild adventure with his father's dog, Jim Ugly, to find out the true story behind his father's disappearance.

George Washington's Breakfast
by Jean Fritz
A young boy named George Washington Allen wanted to learn everything about the first president, including what he ate for breakfast.

There's an Owl in the Shower
by Jean Craighead George
When Borden Watson's father loses his logging job due to spotted owl conservation efforts, the boy swears revenge against this species of bird. But what will the family do when they realize the injured owlet they've been lovingly caring for is actually a spotted owl?

Old Yeller by Fred Gipson
With his father away on a cattle drive, young Travis takes in a frisky dog named Old Yeller to help protect his family on the Texas frontier.

Sarah, Plain and Tall by Patricia MacLachlan
In response to a newspaper ad, a schoolteacher named Sarah moves from Maine to the plains of Kansas to be a wife and mother.

The Cricket in Times Square by George Selden
A cricket named Chester finds a new home at a subway station newsstand in Times Square, New York City.

Roughing It on the Oregon Trail
by Diane Stanley
Two adventurous twins travel back in time to join the pioneers heading west on the Oregon Trail.

The Boxcar Children by Gertrude Warner
Four orphans turn an abandoned boxcar into a home and learn to live on their own.

Charlotte's Web by E.B. White
A wise spider named Charlotte befriends Wilbur the pig. By spinning messages into her web, Charlotte shows everyone just how special Wilbur is.

SUMMER ACTIVITIES AND PROJECTS

Beautiful Bubbles

Blowing bubbles is a great way to spend an afternoon. You can make your own bubble solution by mixing $\frac{1}{4}$ of cup liquid detergent, $\frac{3}{4}$ cup of water, and $1\frac{1}{2}$ tablespoons of light corn syrup. Use a straw, whisk, or cookie cutter to form beautiful, shiny bubbles!

A Cool Treat

You can cool off on a hot summer day with this special recipe for ice cream sandwiches. Choose your favorite type of ice cream and two cookies. Spread the ice cream on one cookie and then put the other cookie on top. Put the whole sandwich in the freezer for a few hours, then enjoy!

Creating Chalk

Creating colorful, life-size pictures is easy when your canvas is as big as a sidewalk! Use colored chalk to draw on the sidewalk. You can even make your own colored chalk by mixing 1 cup of plaster of paris, 1 cup of water, and powdered tempura paint. Pour the mixture into a mold (such as a toilet paper tube) and let it dry for 72 hours. Cleaning up is easy, too. Just pour water over the sidewalk and your pictures will wash away.

Family Flag

Make a family flag! Come up with a design that represents your whole family. Decorate the flag with pictures, symbols, phrases, or important dates that tell about your family.

Fun with Fossils

Make your own fossils! Gather up some objects like leaves, coins, and shells. Then press each object into a small mound of clay or dough. When the clay dries, you'll be able to see the imprint. This is how fossils are formed!

Get into Shape

Get into shape by creating your own obstacle course. Be creative as you set up your course! You can hop through old tires, jump over boxes, or run around cones. Time yourself and see if you can beat your own record.

Make Your Own Sock Puppets!

Don't just throw away your old, mismatched socks. Make sock puppets! Use markers to draw faces. Sew on buttons for eyes and old yarn for hair. After you've finished a few puppets, you can stage a puppet show for your family!

My First Journal

You'll want to remember all your summer adventures when you're older, so start your own journal. Find a notebook and decorate the cover. Use your journal to write about your feelings or to draw pictures.

A New Pet

How about adding a new pet to your family? There's one type of pet that your parents will definitely let you bring home—a pet rock! Find a rock outside and decorate it with art supplies. You can even have a pet rock parade with your friends!

Puzzle Pieces

Make your own puzzle! Find a magazine cover or large picture that can be cut up. You could even use a copy of a photograph you like. On the back side of the picture, trace a pattern of puzzle pieces. Then use scissors to cut along your lines. Mix up the pieces and put the puzzle together.

ANSWER KEY

Page 6
2. fight; face
3. right; race
4. plight; place
5. bright; brace
6. t(ight)rope
7. alr(ight)
8. firepl|ace|
9. ton(ight)
10. shoel|ace|
11. gr|ace|ful
12. fr(ight)ened
13. pl|ace|mat

Page 7
1. b
2. c
3. false
4. true
5. false
6. true

Page 8
2. 9,076; ones; 2,906
3. 6,203; thousands; 6,909
4. 1,068; tens; 9,468
6. 1,000 + 700 + 40 + 3
7. 5,214
8. 9,000 + 300 + 20 + 4
9. 8,152
10. 6,000 + 500 + 30 + 9

Page 9
2. 60
3. 420
4. 6,550
5. 850
6. 700
7. 700
8. 8,200
9. 1,400
10. 100
12. 4,000
13. 3,000
14. 7,000
15. 1,000

Page 10
1. Chicago
2. Dallas
3. Detroit
4. Houston
5. Los Angeles
6. New York City
7. Philadelphia
8. Phoenix
9. San Antonio
10. San Diego
11. New York City
12. Los Angeles
13. Chicago
14. Houston
15. Philadelphia
16. Phoenix
17. San Diego
18. Dallas
19. San Antonio
20. Detroit

Page 11
Possible answers include:
Solids: balloon, drinking
    fountain, cart, tent
Liquids: water, soda, milk
Gases: helium, steam

Page 12
<u>Dear</u> Grandma,
I just got the card you __sent__ me for my birthday. Yesterday I turned __eight__ years old. We went on a hike __through__ the woods. It was a beautiful day, and the __scent__ of wildflowers was in the air. We even saw a __deer__ ! We came to a __creek__ with clear, __blue__ water. As we walked across the bridge, I heard it __creak__ . At lunchtime, we stopped for a picnic and __ate__ sandwiches and chips. We __threw__ away all our trash. When we got home, I __blew__ out the candles on my birthday cake. I wished that I could go on another hike for my birthday next year!
1. clothes
2. red
3. bear
4. new
5. pair

Page 13
2. 1
3. 2
4. 4
5. b
6. b
7. Answers will vary.

Page 14
1. 1,039
2. 82
3. 889
4. 142
5. 988
6. 114
7. 3,999
8. 2,120
9. 4,708
10. 2,111

Page 15

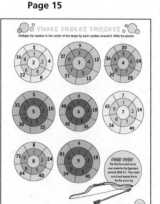

Page 16
1. Shady Way
   and Sandstorm Trail
2. Paradise Passage
3. Rocky Road
4. Sandstorm Trail
5. Paradise Peaks
6. Big Trout River
7. Shady Way
8. Sandstorm Trail

Page 17
2. Light travels in
   a straight line.
3. Sunlight contains all the
   colors of the rainbow.
4. Sunlight can be blocked
   to create shadows.

Page 18
2. un
3. re
4. un
5. dis
6. un
7. re
8. dis
9. dis
10. e
11. f
12. g
13. i
14. c
15. d
16. b
17. h
18. a

Page 19
Present tense:
We go camping every summer. Everyone always helps put up the tent. We like to stay up late and tell stories.

Past tense:
We were all fast asleep inside our tent. Suddenly, I heard a growling noise outside the tent. I shouted, "It's a bear!" Then I heard my brother laughing outside the tent. It was just him!

Page 20
2. 5 x 2 = 10; 2 x 5 = 10;
   5 x 2 = 2 x 5
3. 7 x 5 = 35; 5 x 7 = 35;
   7 x 5 = 5 x 7
4. 6 x 4 = 24; 4 x 6 = 24;
   6 x 4 = 4 x 6
5. 7 x 8 = 56; 8 x 7 = 56;
   7 x 8 = 8 x 7
6. 9 x 3 = 27; 3 x 9 = 27;
   9 x 3 = 3 x 9

Page 21
2. ÷
3. ÷
4. ÷
5. x
6. x
7. ÷
8. ÷

Page 22
2. then
3. now
4. now
5. now
6. then

Page 23
2. koala bear
3. turtle
4. porcupine
5. skunk
6. elephant

Page 24
1. big, bitter
2. bill; Sentences will vary.
3. bill, bite
4. biscuit, bitter
5. bid, blame
6. bin; biscuit
7. Sentences will vary.
8. birth, blade, black, bike

Page 25
1. 1
2. Answers will vary.
3. 4, 8
4. 10
5. c
6. a

Page 26
2. $\frac{4}{6}$
3. $\frac{2}{10}$
4. $\frac{3}{6}$
5. $\frac{2}{8}$
6. $\frac{3}{9}$
7. $\frac{4}{10}$
8. $\frac{2}{12}$
10. P
11. I
12. P
13. P

Page 27
2. $\frac{7}{10}$; .7
3. $\frac{2}{10}$; .2
4. $\frac{1}{4} = \frac{25}{100}$; .25
5. $\frac{2}{4} = \frac{50}{100}$; .50
6. $\frac{3}{4} = \frac{75}{100}$; .75

Page 28
1. b
2. a
3. c
4. c, a, d, b

Page 29
2. true
3. false
4. true
5. false
6. true

Page 30
2. c
3. g
4. h
5. a
6. d
7. e
8. b
9. gentle; rough
10. loud; quiet
11. asleep; awake
12. far; near

Page 31
If you want to have a great summer, spend a week at our camp in Portland, Oregon. The first day of camp this year is Saturday, June 30. Camp runs all summer until Wednesday, August 15.
People have been coming to Camp Comma for years! A small campground was opened here on June 1, 1955. People came to enjoy the hiking, waterfalls, and fishing. Then, on April 20, 1980, Carl Comma decided to open a camp for kids. Now kids come from all over the country to enjoy Camp Comma. We have kids from San Diego, California, and even Fairbanks, Alaska.
   When you come to Camp Comma, don't forget to bring a sleeping bag, a flashlight, and a bathing suit.
   The deadline to enroll for camp is Friday, April 26. Don't wait!

Page 32
2. isosceles
3. equilateral
4. equilateral
5. scalene
6. isosceles
7. isosceles
8. scalene
9. Answers will vary.
10. Answers will vary.

Page 33
2. parallelogram
3. rhombus
4. square
5. rectangle
6. rhombus

Page 34
1. h
2. a

3. g
4. c
5. b
6. f
7. e
8. d

Page 35
2. d
3. b
4. a

Page 36
2. bunnies
3. peaches
4. strawberries
5. napkins
6. cups
7. babies
8. bugs
9. sandwiches
10. sodas

Page 37
1. b
2. c
3. b
4. Answers will vary.
5. Answers will vary.
6. Answers will vary.

Page 38
2. obtuse
3. acute
4. obtuse
5. acute
6. right
7. b

Page 39
2. 5; 0
3. 5; 0
4. 1; 1
5. 2; 1
6. 0; 1

Page 40
2. d
3. a
4. b
5. Oval Office
6. Cabinet Room
7. State Dining Room
8. Blue Room

Page 41
Answers will vary.

Page 42
These are the corrected sentences:
1. Tim and Bill like lots of cheese.
3. Everyone gets his or her own drink.
4. The waiter brings a big salad for everyone to share.
5. Bill wants mushrooms on the pizza.
7. All the kids want pepperoni.

Page 43
2. your
3. they're
4. there
5. your
6. There
7. They're
8. their
9. your
10. There
11. They're
12. your
13. You're
14. you're
15. your
16. their

Page 44
1. 82
2. 36
3. 91
4. 47
5. 282
6. 408
7. 381
8. 227
9. 3,581
10. 3,328
The red car wins

Page 45
2. $21.00
3. 4
4. 3
5. beach towel and floppy hat
6. $7.25

Page 46

• TIMELINE •				
1706	1731	1744	1751	1776
Ben Franklin was born in **Boston**.	Started the first public **library**.	Invented the **Franklin** Stove.	Helped start the **Philadelphia** Academy.	Signed the **Declaration** of **Independence**.

Page 47
2. O
3. E
4. O
5. E
6. c

Page 48
Taste: I bit into a juicy slice of watermelon and enjoyed the sweet flavor.
Touch: I ran my fingers through the soft fur of a goat.
Sound: I heard a crackling sound and then a loud boom.
Sight: I watched as the dark sky exploded with beautiful colors.
The answers at the bottom of the page will vary.

Page 49
2. Atlanta; Georgia
3. Christmas
4. Independence Day
5. Fourth; July
6. American
7. Revolutionary War
8. The Star-Spangled Banner
9. Washington, DC
10. July

Page 50

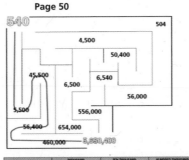

	THOUSAND	TEN THOUSAND	HUNDRED THOUSAND
385,990	386,000	390,000	400,000
712,183	712,000	710,000	700,000
149,230	149,000	150,000	100,000
534,769	535,000	530,000	500,000

Page 51
2. ○ ; ○ ; ▲
3. ■ ; ■ ; ◆ ; ▲
4. 15; 25; 30; 40
5. 10; 16
6. b; c; a; c

Page 52
1. California
2. Idaho
3. Oregon
4. Arizona

Page 53
1. mouse; rabbit; caterpillar
2. hawk; snake; frog

Predator		Prey	
frog		caterpillar	
snake		mouse	frog
hawk		rabbit	
hawk	snake	mouse	

Page 54
1. a
2. b
3. a
4. b
5. b
6. a

Page 55
Answers will be similar to these:
1. I went on vacation with my mom, dad, and sister Amy.
2. We drove down the California coast and stopped in San Francisco, Santa Barbara, and San Diego.
3. It was a long drive, so I read a book and listened to the radio.
4. In San Francisco we saw the Golden Gate Bridge and went to a museum.
5. I swam in the ocean in Santa Barbara with Amy and Mom.
6. San Diego was my favorite place because I liked the zoo.
7. We saw monkeys, gorillas, and apes.
8. Amy liked the tigers the best, but I thought the tigers were too scary.

Page 56
6 x 1 = 6; 1 x 6 = 6
2 x 3 = 6; 3 x 2 = 6
The factors of 6 are 1, 2, 3, 6.

Page 57

Page 58
2. 5°S 10°W
3. 5°S 10°E
4. 5°N 5°E

Page 59
2. urban
3. forest
4. freshwater
5. grassland
6. coastal
7. urban
8. freshwater

Page 60
5; 7; 2; 3; 6; 1; 8; 4

Page 61
2. can't
3. she'll
4. doesn't
5. we're
6. isn't
7. she's
8. hasn't
9. Jim's
10. Dad's

Page 62
1. Perimeter = 5 + 3 + 5 + 3 = 16 cm
   Area = 5 x 3 = 15 cm²
2. Perimeter = 6 + 5 + 6 + 5 = 22 in
   Area = 6 x 5 = 30 in²
3. Perimeter = 18 ft
   Area = 14 ft²
4. Perimeter = 16 cm
   Area = 16 cm²
5. Perimeter = 18 inches
   Area = 8 in²

Page 63
1. 172,885
2. 428,120
3. 121,030
4. 221,212
5. 469,300
6. 186,014
7. 2,250
8. 963
9. 698
10. 365
11. 652
12. 635

Page 64
2. senator
3. representative
4. president
5. representative
6. senator

Page 65
1. insects, animals, water
2. 3, 2, 4, 1, 5

Page 66
1. Passage B: fiction
2. Passage A: Modern-day chewing gum
   was invented by accident.
   Passage B: Betty wanted
   to make the biggest bubble ever.
3. Answers will vary.

Page 67
2. dictionary
3. encyclopedia
4. almanac
5. card catalog
6. thesaurus
7. index
8. atlas

Page 68
A PIE IN THE SKY

Page 69
1. $1\frac{1}{4}$
2. $1\frac{2}{3}$
3. $1\frac{2}{5}$
4. $1\frac{2}{6}$
5. $\frac{2}{3}$; $1\frac{2}{3}$
6. $\frac{1}{2}$; $1\frac{1}{2}$
7. $\frac{5}{5}+\frac{1}{5}$; $1\frac{1}{5}$
8. $\frac{5}{5}+\frac{3}{5}$; $1\frac{3}{5}$

Page 70
2. constitution
3. governor
4. citizens
5. vote
6. budget
7. taxes
8. educational
9. laws
10. mansion

Page 71

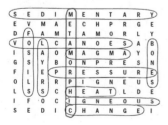

Page 72
2. personification
3. simile
4. simile
5. simile
6. metaphor
7. personification
8. metaphor
The answers at the bottom
of the page will vary.

Page 73
Nouns: settlers, journey, trip
Verbs: started, traveled, was
Adjectives: challenging, big, dusty
Adverbs: bravely, quickly, courageously

Page 74
1. Joe owes 2 dollars; -2
2. Joe owes 4 dollars; -4
3. Joe owes 3 dollars; -3
4. Joe owes 4 dollars; -4
5. Joe owes 2 dollars; -2
6. Joe owes 3 dollars; -3

Page 75
2. 2
3. 2
4. 4
5. 4
6. 6
7. 3
8. 6
9. 6
10. 4
11. 7
12. 6
13. $2
14. $5
15. $10
16. $9
17. $20
18. $101
19. $57
20. $11
21. $96
22. $26
23. $18
24. $87

Page 76

Page 77

Answers may vary slightly.

Page 78
 2 scoops vanilla ice cream
 1 cup milk
 3 tablespoons chocolate syrup
2. false
3. true
4. false
5. false
6. true

Page 79

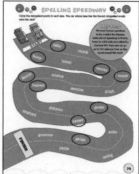

The green car wins.

Page 80
1. 74,240
2. 46, 575
3. 130,040
4. 27,346
5. 99,544
6. 53,400
7. 130,536
8. 103,501
9. 35,695
10. 29,172
LET'S PLAN IT!

Page 81
Slide 1:
1. 42
2. 63
3. 33 R1
4. 64 R1
5. 21 R2

Slide 2:
1. 42
2. 54 R1
3. 321
4. 87 R2
5. 104
Slide 2 is faster.

Page 82
2. Legislative
3. Executive
4. Judicial
5. Legislative
6. Executive

Page 83
2. glacial erosion
3. water erosion
4. wind erosion

Page 84
Answers will vary.

Page 85
1. b
2. c
3. b
4. b
5. a
6. 5, 1, 3, 2, 6, 4

Page 86

1. Main Street
2. Windy Lane
3. Elm Street and Pinewood Avenue
4. 4
5. 6
6. 26

Page 87
Because people were always
POINTING at him!

Page 88

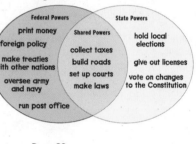

Page 89
2. true
3. false
4. true
5. false
6. false
7. true
8. false

Page 90
Answers will vary.

Page 91
Answers will vary.